CULTURE INFUSION

9 PRINCIPLES TO CREATE AND MAINTAIN A THRIVING ORGANIZATIONAL CULTURE

BY

KERRY ALISON WEKELO

ACCOLADES FOR KERRY ALISON WEKELO

"In my own family's business and now at Actualize Consulting, I've seen how important it is for key leaders to grow a culture that attracts and retains both employees and customers. At Actualize, I have watched Kerry build that culture. Both [Actualize Founding Partner] Chad and I are proud of what Actualize is all about and we couldn't have done it without the unique focus on personal and team growth and achievement that Kerry has created."

—Matt Seu, Partner, Actualize Consulting

"I have never met someone like Kerry in my professional life working for ten companies in three different countries in the past twenty years. In my first two years at Actualize, she has helped and inspired me to do so much, such as going through a detox process; getting back into reading, exercising, and meditation; and participating in charity events. When we had a conflict in my team, she stepped in, and with one hour of conversation the issue was over and the team was happy, ready to move forward and continue to contribute and work together. It is truly inspiring having Kerry around. The world needs more people like her."

—Priscila Nagalli, Senior Manager, Actualize Consulting

Culture Infusion

"As I prepare to start my contract with a new client, I'm admittedly nervous about balancing my brain work and heart/soul work. But I have the *Culture Infusion* book fresh in my mind, and am realizing I'm holding those concepts and Kerry's example as the light of 'You can do this!'"

—**Starla J. King, Editor and Author of** *Wide Awake.*
Every Day: Daily Inspiration for Conscious Living

"When I first came to Actualize Consulting, I instantly bonded with Kerry, and she has become a great mentor to me. She helps guide me towards tasks I enjoy and that bring about my passion and creativity. I'm lucky to work with someone who truly cares about my future in all aspects and provides motivation to be my best."

—**Laura E. Hornick, Senior Consultant, Actualize Consulting**

"The people I work with at Actualize are kind and honest, and they genuinely care about one another. I am most motivated by the culture of the company as it allows me the freedom to think differently, try new approaches, and put my personal stamp on my work."

—**Darren Zuckerman, Director, Actualize Consulting**

"The support I receive at Actualize from all levels of the company is unparalleled. The owners take an active interest in enriching the careers of their employees. The HR department is extremely responsive to every inquiry that comes their way, and our HR staff facilitates recurring internal training initiatives that improve each individual's personal life and career. The culture is built around the attitude that we're all on the same team and we're all in this together."

—**Jean Ballard, Manager, Actualize Consulting**

"As a mentor, Kerry has inspired me to look for answers with a people-centric approach. Kerry's insights have provided me with the tools I use to collaborate, build consensus, and foster a sense of community within all levels of an organization—whether that be with my immediate team or to help me rise to meet the needs of the entire company."

—**Christian Reed, Sr. Total Rewards Manager, CastLight Health**

"Kerry's professionalism, energy, and enthusiasm have created a culture at Actualize that fosters commitment to the firm's mission and drives the best out of the employees. Because the majority of our firm's employees are out in the field 100 percent of the time, she is always coming up with fun, energetic, and meaningful activities that allow employees to get together and spend quality time together. I love the fact that I can always count on Kerry's support and valuable feedback and guidance no matter the issue."

—**John Pomranski, Senior Manager, Actualize Consulting**

"Over the past ten years, Kerry's transformation has been nothing less than spectacular. From a very effective manager, a kind person, and a great Mom who had a significant impact on all around her, to someone who creates meaningful change in the world. Purposeful, positive, and proactive. Kerry's influence on making the world a better place has grown exponentially, at a time when it is more important than ever."

—**John Harvey, Founder, T2Partners/TransitionWorks**

For Angela Dawn (Smith) Ruoto

My childhood best friend who inspired living life as a magical adventure filled with love, play, laughter, and creativity. She advocated that I always live a life wide open and I dedicate this book and special poem to her memory.

Wide Open

Listen with an open heart.
Follow the rhythm of the beats.

Steady and slow—slow and steady.
Listen to understand.
Listen with compassion.

Do you hear the rhythm of the words?
The beauty of words when you take time to hear them?

Pause to listen.

Smile to acknowledge your understanding.

The words and heartbeat join in compassion.
Steady and slow—slow and steady.
Words in rhythm.

Heart beating wide open.

Coming together is a beginning.
Keeping together is progress.
Working together is success.
—Henry Ford

TABLE OF CONTENTS

Culture Infusion

ON CULTURE

Culture is more than a word; it is the pulse of your organization, your family, your way of being. In terms of business, we attract talent based on the image and culture of our organization that is visible from the outside. A thriving culture also has a positive effect internally; it creates a positive workplace and keeps our employees happy. To create and maintain a thriving organizational culture, our teams must feel valued and passionately believe in our visions. Else, the culture is humdrum versus pulsing with the excitement to be our best.

While culture is an integral part of any organization, culture starts on a personal, individual level. Our own personal story shapes how we show up in all aspects of our lives. If we are out of balance and unclear about our desires (in our personal lives *or* at work), how will we be able to lead our teams effectively? *Culture Infusion* is for leaders and aspiring leaders who want to build a legacy, shift perspectives, and lead by example so others are inspired and driven to be their best selves. Whether you are a top-level executive or lead a team, you will find valuable insights in this book on how to create and maintain a sought-after workplace. You'll learn how to infuse culture in all aspects of your organization, from your people to your programs, and how we must thrive personally in order to lead others. In his simple yet powerful statement "You must be the change you wish to see in the world," Mahatma Gandhi suggests we lead by example. If we wish to see change, we must first start within. Each moment, action, and word is a commitment to lead with our heart and add value to the world. Each one of us can leave our mark by taking accountability for creating and maintaining a thriving organizational culture.

A Holistic Approach

This book is not your standard business how-to book. Instead of presenting a siloed approach to improving an organizational culture, it presents a holistic approach that is built on a broader foundation of personal wellness. I present, based on my own proven experience, nine principles I have used in my personal life and as the Managing Director of Human Resources and Operations at Actualize Consulting. Consider me and Actualize your case study, sharing what I have learned so you and your organization can benefit without going through quite as many growing pains.

When I made the decision to commit to my own personal growth, it became clear to me that all aspects of our lives are connected. At first, I was under the impression it had to be either/or: either personal *or* business. I had a vision of choosing the personal focus—leaving my job at Actualize Consulting in order to teach yoga, meditation, and mindfulness full-time. In reality, that was not a financially feasible option for me as a single mom, nor did that idea feel good or wise. I was not willing to walk away from this company that I'd grown to love as one of my children. I also was not willing to leave my brother, Chad, the founder of Actualize. Even though he is only a year and a half younger than I am, I have always taken care of my little brother, and supporting him continues to be important to me. I knew I needed to also focus on myself and my work, so I wanted to be in a place where I could care for myself, my work, *and* my brother.

As I focused on my desire to have meaningful relationships and experiences in all aspects of my life, I realized that compartmentalization of my values was *not* an option. I needed a holistic approach to, well, everything. I needed to show up as the same person in all aspects of my life so I could serve myself and others for our highest good. This meant I would have to find a way to help form a more holistic approach to success at Actualize—one that encouraged personal and corporate wellness in all aspects, from physical and mental well-being to "healthy," well-functioning operations. I wanted to take to heart Kahlil Gibran's thoughts on work in his book *The Prophet*: "Work is love made visible." He goes on to say, "And if you cannot work with love and only distaste, it is better you should leave your work and sit at the gate of the temple and take alms of those who work with joy."[1] I wanted to create a culture and workplace that made me and others proud to call Actualize our place of work.

From a macro perspective, my personal approach was guided by the 3A's (in Principle 6, I will explain these 3A's in detail as they apply to the corporate setting):

- **Accountability:** Each party takes honest accountability in each situation

- **Acumen:** All involved hone skills to strengthen and grow personally and as a team

- **Aspiration:** We choose our path based on what is of most interest and excites us at a personal level, and we support others' aspirations

Upon further reflection, I saw that these principles I was applying to my personal leadership would translate to my approach with my kids, friends, family, *and* work. No matter who or what is the end focus, it all starts at the individual level. The first step is having the courage to personally take care of our own needs. Once our own needs are met, we are able to successfully integrate the personal lessons at a corporate (or any other) level. In this book, we explore how over the years Actualize Consulting has thrived with a holistic approach to integrating a culture of positivity, learning, and success into all aspects of our business.

We took our time and slowly and steadily infused some key principles into our corporate culture. If you are looking for any or all of the following for yourself, your team, and/or your organization, then this book is worth your time:

- Improve corporate culture

- Lead by positive example

- Motivate employees

- Increase retention, job satisfaction, and morale

- Enhance individual and team performance and overall working experience

- Gain resulting benefits such as higher-quality talent attracted to your organization and increased customer satisfaction

- Merge companies or teams or manage through transitions

- Be a change agent for a culture where people want to work

The thriving culture at Actualize Consulting is built on a solid foundation of personal wellness, expanded into team interactions and corporate structure and operations. This book takes you behind the scenes of how my team and I created this culture, and how you can also create a thriving culture.

9 Principles of a Thriving Organizational Culture

Principle 1: Provide intentional leadership

Principle 2: Prioritize personal wellness

Principle 3: Insist on a healthy work/life balance

Principle 4: Practice effective communication

Principle 5: Handle conflict directly, openly, and immediately

Principle 6: Focus on your people

Principle 7: Regularly conduct employee surveys

Principle 8: Align goals to rewarding performance

Principle 9: Encourage team connection

HOW TO USE THIS BOOK

Before digging into each of the nine principles, I share a very condensed version of my own personal and professional journey—the journey that led to this book. I believe each experience teaches us lessons, so I share the key lessons I learned from growing up in a family business and how personal growth helped me create a clearer vision of myself as a leader.

The nine principles build on each other, so I recommend you read them in order. However, if you need some ideas and recommendations about a particular principle, you will still get plenty of usable information even if you skip around. You can always come back to previous principles at a later time.

Take your time with each principle, allowing the concepts to sink in so you can more easily integrate them into your personal and corporate life. Also take time to answer the questions throughout the book and do the exercises in the Mind-Expanding Experiences section at the end of each chapter, which are designed to guide your learning. Whether you decide to handwrite your thoughts in a journal or type them on a computer, take the time to go inward. That's where success begins.

MIND-EXPANDING EXPERIENCE

How do you prefer to capture your learning and reflections: writing in a journal, or typing your thoughts on computer? Before you begin this journey, secure a place to write or type your thoughts (set aside a designated notebook or writing pages, or start a new document on your computer).

CULTURAL BEGINNINGS

Each of us has our unique life story that shapes who we are, how we show up, and how we look at and feel our way through life. All the moments from small to large leave imprints that mold our essence. To give you a more complete background on the principles of this book, I start with the uncomfortable truth of how my path led me to compiling a book on culture.

First, it is vital to note that I am a sensitive person. This is relevant because until recently, I did not realize my true essence nor the gifts of being sensitive and intuitive. I felt out of place and wanted to blend in rather than standing out in fear of others getting too close and seeing my true self. As a sensitive being, I have wanted to hide, and honestly many days I do hide. But the days when I interact, spread love and compassion fully, and contently listen and engage are the days when my heart expands and life flows.

I feel others' energies, notice facial expressions, gauge a look or a crossing of the arms. I see and feel more than I hear. I see your best; I feel your pain. I want from the center of my heart and soul to facilitate a better life for you. For you to see your magnificent purpose in this lifetime. For you to choose in the moment to let go of the past and move forward cherishing each moment. For you to love fully and openly—to love yourself, to forgive yourself, to love others, to forgive others openly and freely—so you flow as eloquently as water flows, moving and forging as nature guides. Forcing that which we desire creates roadblocks and failures that are not fulfilling. I have learned if it does not flow with grace and ease, I need to be patient and let the person, situation, or decision settle while I wait. Eventually, the answer or the solution will magically appear.

For example, one morning as I was writing this book, my computer would not turn on. Instead of getting wrapped up in frustration of what I couldn't do, I instead focused on what I *could* do. I used the space created by not being able to use my computer and practiced yoga by my teacher Rolf Gates, then followed it with reading and meditation. Then I pulled an angel card by Doreen Virtue. The card was titled "Sensitivity" and the message read, "Your sensitive feelings are your muse and inspiration for your creativity." I took a few moments of quiet on my mat and discovered the flow of words and insights that you are reading now. The words in this book would not be possible without my sensitivity to you and to the world, which allows flow and ongoing innovation as I stay in each moment of truth. The sensitivity is the golden ticket to seeing, feeling, and hearing those who are traveling by my side and on a similar path.

The greatest lesson I have personally learned and seen my peers experience is following this path of contentment, aiming to touch joy in any circumstance, seeing the positive, and flowing towards the peace and harmony of *what is* and saying to ourselves, "And so it is." My personal motto, "living life in adventure and wonder," is inspired by Helen Keller. Ever since childhood, I have been in awe of her strength and courage to make a beautiful life even though she was both deaf and blind. Because of her limited senses, the ones she did have were more powerful, and she refused to focus on the senses that she lacked. I echo her belief that "life is either a daring adventure or nothing at all." Like Helen, I am not satisfied with humdrum. "Everything has its wonders," she wrote in *The Story of My Life*, "even darkness and silence, and I learn whatever state I may be in, therein to be content."[2] It is a daily practice for me to do my best to be content with how I am able to show up each day—the good, the bad, and the ugly. Each day, each year, the practice of contentment comes more easily to me.

My brother, Chad, and I spent much of our childhood on my grandparents' farm in Virginia's Shenandoah Valley. To this day, as I travel down the road to my childhood home, I slip into a place of peace. I believe that nature has been one of my most influential teachers. Nature flows, allows, and breezes through its seasons, but is also a force to be taken seriously. One of my first lessons of this was when our beloved and tranquil river flooded, destroying the land, lifting the bridge, and taking my mother's car. The river's lesson? That there are both calm and stormy times, and even in the hardest times, nature will flow season by season and year by year. There is beauty in each and every moment if we pause to witness a flower blooming, a river's soothing flow, and each miracle bestowed upon us.

Fast forward from my idyllic childhood to the spring of 2010. From the outside looking in, I had the perfect life: an amazing and supportive husband, two beautiful kids, and a successful career. We, too, were living the dream. Or so it appeared.

One morning as I was driving my daughter, Audrey, to preschool, I causally listened to a voicemail from Dawn, a childhood friend. She always called with a cheerful message, so I assumed her voicemail today would leave me laughing, and I was surprised to hear her words: "Kerry, *call me*, Sadie is in the hospital, and she is unconscious. She tried to kill herself!"

My heart was racing as my thoughts went into overdrive. *I need to go see Sadie...what about the kids? Sadie was the friend I counted on to be happy, uplifting, and positive—how could this have happened? What about work...UGH, work!* As I made the drive home to the Valley, my sacred space, I was overwhelmed with questions. *Why on earth would she try to kill herself? She seemed so happy. Why would she want to leave us?* And on and on went the conversation in my head.

By the time I arrived, Sadie had regained consciousness and had been moved to the psych ward for observation. By the grace of a higher power, Sadie was given a second chance. I held back tears, mustering the power to remain calm and strong, and asked her, "Sadie, why?"

"Kerry, it is bad, bad, and really bad. I should have died. I want to die. It is bad...bad...bad."

"But you are here now," I responded, "and that is a gift."

"Kerry, it's *BAD, BAD*..."

I squeezed Sadie's hand. "But you are alive, you have a second chance, we can get through this." I said it, praying it was true.

In the days, weeks, and months to follow, I was often distraught and sad. Sadie was usually so positive. How could I have missed her signs of unhappiness? Tragedy takes us deep within ourselves. The near death of this dear and sweet friend left me pondering life, wondering what was the truth, if the happiness she had portrayed was a lie.

I had already added yoga to my routine by this time, so I was able to find comfort on my yoga mat, and I found solitude on my walks and runs in nature. With the time to reflect and slow down to focus on my physical body, a voice began to speak to me. "Kerry, you are no different. You are living the same lie. You are not happy in your marriage and nobody knows. From the outside looking in, you are just like Sadie, and it appears that you have the perfect life." The voice kept getting louder and louder. "What are you going to do about it?"

I decided to end my marriage, even though nobody other than my husband and I knew that we should not be married. We had never disclosed that there were any issues, so the mention of divorce shocked our family and friends. The details are irrelevant here; we just could not love each other the way the other needed to be loved. We divorced, but to this day we have an amazing co-parenting relationship and remain life partners.

With the divorce, for once in my life, I had the freedom to choose my path, to make my own decisions. I promised myself I would do my best to speak the truth and live the life I wanted and deserved. And so, began a journey of self-reflection and self-awareness. I read books, completed 500 hours of yoga training, and worked with numerous mentors and coaches. Life got easier, and the natural peace I had as a child returned. I took time to be in awe of nature, and I was taking better care of myself. I realized when I took time for myself and met all my needs, I was happier in all facets of life. I was not spinning in the details; I was going with the flow as nature does.

The first step in courage was leaving my marriage. The second step was to leave my job or find the courage to stand up for making my workplace a better place to work. My boss just happened to be my brother, Chad. Our parents divorced when I was five years old and Chad was four, and having divorced parents was simply our way of life. Our mom had full custody of us and worked full-time. Our father lived in various cities until we were in high school when he settled in Richmond, Virginia, where he still lives today. As I reflect on our childhood, I realize we were exposed to more than our friends were, and were given high levels of responsibility at an early age. While quite young, we were witness to family and corporate parties that were not suitable for kids.

From the beginning, we took care of each other while building a foundation of trust. There are countless stories of Chad and me supporting one another. I remember when I was in the fourth grade, we were consistently hungry before our mom could get home to make dinner, so I took it upon myself to learn how to cook. Chad was always in my math class, even though he was one year behind me in school, so he would tutor me in math. Since our closest neighbors with kids were over a mile away, we would take turns playing Barbies/School and He-Man/Sports together. We learned at an early age the value of compromise and give and take. With the bond we shared, there were also daily fights. One time after returning from college, when Chad finally was taller and stronger than I, our discussion got heated and he threw me into a cabinet so hard that I suffered a mild concussion.

We learned of business and hard work from spending time at our family's manufacturing business. I started working during the summers at the age of five and continued through college. I started with pulling weeds, making copies, and taking inventory, and ended up performing every function within the company at some point. I had completed the equivalent of a hands-on Business 101 course before I even started college!

Culture Infusion

As I embarked on the new territory of college, I knew one thing for sure: I would not be joining the family business after graduation. The fighting, bickering, and backstabbing was not a culture I wanted to be part of. So, after graduating with a dual major in Finance and Marketing and a minor in Psychology, I joined the prestigious firm Anderson Consulting (now Accenture). Consulting was a perfect fit for me, given my diverse accumulated skill set, ability to get along with others, and desire to be the best. After Accenture, I worked for a few other consulting firms and corporations. At every job, I was identified as a quick learner with the ability to complete any task no matter the difficulty.

Chad was the founding partner of Actualize, LLC, a consulting firm in Northern Virginia. When he asked me to join Actualize to help him build out the internal operations of the firm, I quickly said yes because I knew I would be successful and was up for the challenge of a new venture. Our family cautioned us, given our track record of fighting, yet we both knew in our hearts—even though we didn't say it out loud—that we trusted each other 100 percent.

That was in May 2005, and I have been with Actualize ever since. I joke with recruits that I have three children: Actualize; my daughter, Audrey (born October 2005); and my son, Blaine (born March 2008). When my children were born, Actualize was still in start-up mode, so I did not take a proper maternity leave with either child. That being said, I have the huge advantage of being able to mainly work from home and have had extreme flexibility in being a present parent for all three of my children.

Actualize has been profitable and successful each year of operation, and over the years we have built a reputation and culture that is known in our industry and that recruits seek out. I believe there are several reasons for our success: 1) I have no ownership in the firm, which creates an important division of power—ultimately, my brother is the decision maker, unlike in our family's business, where the main issue is no division and ongoing struggles for power; 2) we strive to put our people first and to provide exceptional client service; and 3) Chad and I trust each other and respect each other's unique gifts.

With our success, there have been cultural struggles along the way. As I mentioned earlier, after taking the first step of courage to leave my marriage, I was ready to take the second step. I told my brother I wanted to leave the firm because I did not believe it was a good place to work, mainly due to strife among the management team on how to run the business, which was trickling down to our teams. Ethically, I could not recruit talent to join us and honestly say it was an exceptional culture. Chad talked me into staying and agreed that we would work on the management issues.

Around that time, a friend gave me the book *Leadership and Self-Deception: Getting Out of the Box* by the Arbinger Institute. An avid reader, I immediately read the book. It is an excellent story of how we all must take accountability in each situation, acknowledging that there are always two sides of an issue. We all contribute to any conflicts and negative emotions we are feeling by staying inside our "box" of being right, so the solution is to get out of that box, to let go of the need to be right. The book summarizes in a business sense all I had been learning on my spiritual path. Jazzed by the concepts I had read, I went to Chad and suggested the management team read the book and conduct a team-building exercise. Chad trusted in the idea and said yes. That was the first step in transforming our culture to create a firm where I am happy to work, that others want to join, and that I am excited to bring new talent into.

We went on to build a foundation of truth and trust at Actualize by adding small "infusions" (manageable positive changes made over time) to our culture over the years. With each new program or change away from the status quo of how to run our business, our teams began to work better together and with more collaboration. Our employee-satisfaction surveys and the tenure of our teams improved. As I started to witness the positive impacts, I was motivated to continue with new programs and changes to the old ways. One of the most impactful changes was related to how we aligned our goal setting and performance reviews around our business and added in personal components. This allowed our teams to focus on their aspirations that aligned with ours. (I will go into more detail on this in Principle 8: Align Goals to Rewarding Performance.)

For this book, I have taken these tried-and-true cultural enhancements or "infusions" we have used at Actualize to create the 9 Principles of a Thriving Organizational Culture. The following chapters are a deep dive into each of these principles, including how to infuse all aspects of your personal and professional life with them.

MIND-EXPANDING EXPERIENCES

Personal

Our own personal story shapes how we show up in all aspects of our lives. Personally, I used to tell a negative story about my life versus appreciating how my story shapes the person I am today and understanding what I can learn from my story and life lessons.

What aspects of your personal story can you change to be more positive?

1. Close your eyes and visualize your story.
2. Free write, starting at the beginning and following whatever comes to mind. Do not worry about grammar or making it perfect.
3. Cross out the most negative section and instead write about the lessons you learned from that experience and how they make you who you are today. What is one thing you are grateful for in regards to your personal story? Write it down.

Team

In a group setting, have your team complete the above exercise, but instead of focusing on their life, ask them what negative story they have been telling themselves or friends and family about work. In the last step, ask them to write down the aspects of work or their job they enjoy and what they are grateful for about your firm. Ask how they can contribute to changing their story to a positive one and have a more enjoyable work experience.

Culture Infusion

To infuse positive thinking into your company, provide opportunities for leaders and team members to publicly share gratitude and appreciation for each other. At Actualize, in our biweekly newsletter we share employee spotlights and success stories and have a section where anyone can share appreciation for others. It is our way to keep positivity flowing.

LIFE LESSONS A CONTRASTING-CULTURE CASE STUDY

It was the beginning of 2015 and I was packing for the next day's particularly important business trip, carefully choosing the right clothing, jewelry, and shoes. I wanted—I *needed*—to walk into the client site and be respected. First, I selected my great-grandmother Pauline's delicate diamond-banded ring. Next, I chose a pair of three-diamond dangling earrings from my Grandmother Gloria and a diamond tennis bracelet from my mother. The last accessory was a personal touch: a necklace holding a sand dollar pendant with the words "Pixie Dust" inscribed on the back. All of these external accessories were reminders of the power I wanted to exude as I walked through the company doors for my new engagement.

I awoke the next morning at 4:00 for yoga and meditation, setting a tone of clarity and confidence to prepare for the day's work. Then, as I made the two-hour drive across Virginia towards my childhood neck of the woods, my emotions fluctuated from nervous and tense to a peaceful place of courage. I continued my positive self-talk, gearing up for what was sure to be no ordinary day. Taking one more deep breath, I pulled into the parking lot of my family's business.

Typically, I would go into my mom's entrance on the left, but on this day, I chose the front entrance to make the visit feel more professional. I took a few deeper breaths and said a prayer that I would be able to assist my family to their good and better.

It felt odd (to say the least) to be at my family business again, this time as an outside consultant. My mother had hired Actualize for practical support when their whole Human Resources department had given two weeks' notice. I was tasked with documenting the processes and procedures, hiring a new team, and ensuring operations remained stable.

My family was focused on the tactical and I was feeling as if time had remained still. As the familiar and comforting smell of metal lingered in the air, I sighed as I scrolled through green screens in sheer amazement that the computer systems had not been upgraded in years. The reams of paper for one new hire made my head spin. I realized that before the company could move forward, it needed to first get current!

I could understand the appeal of keeping things the same for so long, as even I felt nostalgic when seeing familiar faces.

"Darling, good to see you, how long has it been?"

Beaming, I responded, "James! How are you? It's been twenty-plus years, huh?" I have no memory of the family business without James being present in some capacity, and it was nice to see him again.

"Some things never change, darling; I just wish your family would get along. Heck, I don't care, as I know they mean well, but they are running off all the new folk."

I sighed. "That would be why I am here."

"Darling, good luck. Let me know if you need anything; you know I can set you straight." He gave me his cell phone number, truly ready to do anything to be helpful.

"Well, James, it was great to see you again; I'm sure I'll see you around."

He smiled, eyes twinkling, then his handsomely rough and weathered face turned serious. "Kerry, be sure to set your boundaries, you hear?"

"Roger that," I chuckled, even as tears sprang to my eyes. I was (and still am) in awe at the commitment of those, like James, who stood by my family through thick and thin, even as they were "running off all the new folk."

I was curious why the attrition rates of the newer hires were so high, so I dug through the company files, hoping to find some answers. As I reviewed recent employee survey data and exit interview responses, it became clear to me that my mom and her two brothers were still fighting, even after all those years. And as I stayed on-site witnessing the day-to-day operations, I realized that the generational gaps were also an issue impacting attrition.

The new (and younger) teams at my family's business were finding it challenging to work in the old-school systems and processes that in many cases were outdated. The generational gap went deep, and I knew it must be addressed in order for the company to succeed. The first step was educating my family on the differences. Even as I write this, they continue to make small steps in the right direction by empowering their newer staff.

I fulfilled my contractual duties to stabilize operations and hire a new team, I was successful in presenting a business case to upgrade the Human Resources system, and I implemented the upgrade prior to my departure from the project. I felt good about the positive mark I made on the family business.

Comparing what I experienced at my family's business with how things were for me at Actualize, I saw our team and our people in a new light. I was filled with even more gratitude and insight into the culture we had built at Actualize. I came back from that consulting engagement with a clearer vision of the importance of culture and a new determination to keep enhancing ours at Actualize. As a realist, I know that the larger the change we wish for, the longer we must be willing to commit, work, and wait for it, and the experience at my family's business strengthened my resolve for the long haul.

It also became clear to me that my brother and I had broken the cycle of our family drama, using the strength of our relationship to help build a successful and culturally sound business. With the additional strengths of Chad's business partner, Matt, we have shown that family can work together to our advantage and greater good. In fact, when Chad and I recently attended our family's business shareholders meeting, they were impressed by our working relationship, as evidenced by this note from our mom: "I am still floating from yesterday's meeting. I never thought you and Chad would *ever* work together. Yesterday I got to see it in person and it was very impressive. Great answer when I asked how you and Chad work so well together. The simplicity of respect, trust, and working as a team is setting an example for us other three siblings."

I am reminded of the following passage from *Culture Making* by Andy Crouch: "What is the right way to evaluate cultural change?

I suggest integrity."[3] Chad and I have learned the importance of integrity in our own relationship, and we are using that experience to infuse our entire company culture with a positive focus on honesty, openness, and respect. As we are shifting and mentoring this cultural change at Actualize for generations to come, not only will our children and our immediate cousins (whose parents are involved in the family business) see the model, our employees see us setting the tone at the top that our *people* matter most to us.

In this small company of less than 100 people (and just fifty full-time employees), I wear multiple hats and have the luxury of seeing the big picture of all of our operations. This has helped me facilitate a positive cultural shift at Actualize—from addressing how we communicate, to prioritizing wellness, to engaging in positive social activities and events, to enhancing our goal and performance processes.

This book is the result of that cultural shift, and I hope it helps you implement a similar shift and improve your corporate culture.

MIND-EXPANDING EXPERIENCES

Personal

In order to be clear on the person I wanted to be to lead by example, I had to take a look at my family and upbringing. To be our best selves, it can be helpful to examine our past and the learned patterns that have become so comfortable but may not be the example we want to set. Take time to answer the following:

1. How has your family impacted the person you are?

2. What do you want to carry on to the next generation?

3. What cycle do you want to break?

BONUS:

Take one step to break a negative cycle. For example, my family communicates by fighting. I have taken great strides to communicate respectfully rather than fighting, and even if a fight occurs, I quickly apologize for my part. What step will you take?

Team

Understanding our business lessons is also telling. Within a team you would like to see enhance their collaboration and communication, have members brainstorm on the top lessons they have learned in their careers. Next, discuss how to continue those lessons or break the cycle within their current team.

Culture Infusion

Ensure lessons learned are a part of your culture by using a formal lessons-learned process after completion of major firm-wide initiatives. At Actualize, we document lessons learned after each client project is completed.

PRINCIPLE 1

Provide Intentional Leadership

Being extremely honest with oneself is a good exercise.

—Sigmund Freud

There are different schools of thought regarding whether anyone can be groomed to become a successful leader or if only certain people have the predisposition to be successful leaders. In other words, does someone have to be born a leader, or is it possible to train someone to be a leader? The *Forbes* article "Are Leaders Born or Made?"[4] references research that shows that both situations are true, with training having an even greater impact on leadership success than genetics. My personal experience leads to a similarly eclectic conclusion that we are born with innate ways of being, yet our environment also impacts our world view, interpersonal interactions, and our leadership styles. I have found the most success upon the realization that in order to be effective, we need to commit to supporting the growth of people and not just systems, products, or processes.

Where traditional leadership training often falls short is that it begins with a focus on *other* people. I propose that it needs to instead begin with a focus on oneself. How can leaders be truly aware of others if they're not aware of themselves? How can they be wise about the needs of others if they're not wise about their own needs? But true leaders don't focus *only* on themselves. They broaden their circle of care. They inspire and lift others up to their highest potential by looking at them as individuals who each have their own strengths.

Let's commit, as leaders, to understand the personal so we can begin to better understand the interpersonal—the relationships of our teams, our organizations, and our clients.

What Exceptional Leaders Do

Most businesses deal with substantial daily stress from the demands for results under ongoing time pressure. To meet increasing workloads, the most effective leaders spend significant time observing operations. To do this *and maintain the well-being of the people doing the work*, exceptional leaders also need to observe the people, taking time to see each individual and his or her strengths, to be empathetic, and to lead from a place of understanding.

But what exactly do exceptional leaders look for? And how do they implement the right changes based on what they see? They start with observing themselves. Leaders who want to effectively facilitate the well-being of their teams need to first facilitate their own personal well-being. Effective leadership starts with an internal view and self-awareness.

Practice Self-Awareness and Reflection

The first step of self-awareness is to notice and better understand how we tend to justify our behaviors, which can lead to what's called "cognitive dissonance." In their book *Mistakes Were Made (But Not By Me)*, Carol Tavris and Elliot Aronson explain, "Cognitive dissonance is a state of tension that occurs whenever a person holds two cognitions (ideas, attitudes, beliefs, opinions) that are psychologically inconsistent."[5] For example, cognitive dissonance occurs when we drink soda even though we know it is unhealthy for us. To reduce this dissonance, we decide to quit drinking soda. However, if we fail to quit drinking soda, we reduce the dissonance by convincing ourselves that drinking soda really is not that bad for us anyway.

From a leadership perspective, we might bark orders at our team even though deep down we know it is best to ask for collaboration instead. To reduce the dissonance, we justify to ourselves that we are in charge and our team should take orders with no input or opinions.

In addition to being aware of such dissonance and other issues in themselves, the best leaders then extend their self-awareness by noticing how their behaviors and attitudes impact others. Remember the Freud quote from the beginning of this chapter? "Being extremely honest with oneself is a good exercise." If we take time to honestly look at ourselves and our triggers, we can continue to grow. Life is a learning process and we strengthen our development by looking at how we show up.

Defensiveness is a powerful clue to our areas of needed growth. The next time you find yourself reacting negatively, take a moment to analyze why. Most often there is an important truth to uncover. For instance, your staff says you are a micromanager, and every time you are made aware of this you feel your temperature rising and your inner voice says, "I am not a micromanager!" Seasoned leaders see there is some truth in the way others view them and recognize it as an opportunity to improve. They then take the necessary steps to enhance their behavior to improve and empower their team.

An important best practice is to incorporate self-reflection across the organization. At Actualize, we recently added self-reflection on career objectives to our biannual review process. Self-reflections are a powerful way for individuals to become more aware of how they operate, both in a personal and work capacity.

The solution in either case is to focus on changing the unhelpful behavior, not justifying it. How? Start by setting clear intentions.

Set Intentions

Webster's New World Dictionary: Compact School and Office Edition defines *intention* as "the thing that you plan to do or achieve: an aim or purpose." In any facet of life, intentions require us to get clear on our plans and purpose, and then they help keep us focused.

In business, intention setting not only facilitates communication among teams, but also aids us in clarifying the why behind our strategy. When we take time to analyze the intention, we can hone in on a clearer vision, enabling us to explain it to others and obtain organizational buy-in and support.

Tips For Setting And Implementing Effective Intentions

1. Define your intention as clearly as possible.

2. Implement your intention:

   a. Align your thoughts with the intention.

   b. Align your actions according to the intention.

3. Assess effectiveness based on how others view your intentions.

   a. Do they want to work with you, or ask you for advice? If yes, you can conclude others value your guidance.

   b. However, if you are leading with little interaction, you may want to re-evaluate how you are actually impacting others.

For example, a team leader might set and implement an intention as follows:

1. Define intention: *My intention is that we work as a team.*

2. Implement intention:

   a. Align thoughts: *I believe my team will provide a more robust set of ideas for our firm.*

   b. Align actions: *I ask for input on major decisions, and I ask for opinions on a regular basis. I ask people what they recommend when giving me ideas or suggestions.*

3. Assess effectiveness: *Do my team members interact with me, and with each other? Do other teams want to work with my team?*

In his book *The Seat of the Soul*, Gary Zukav says, "The more aware of your intentions and your experiences you become, the more you will be able to connect the two, and the more you will be able to create the experiences of your life consciously. This is the development of mastery. It is the creation of authentic power."[6] Lead intentionally and you, your teams, organizations, and businesses will prosper in ways unimagined.

Create Clarity

Great leaders consistently create and communicate clarity. Think of exceptional leaders you know. Are their plans and purpose murky or clear? Most likely their plans and purpose are exceptionally clear, and the leaders have a focused energy that draws others to them and their cause. How do leaders gain such powerful clarity? As with the other leadership qualities we have discussed so far, they start with themselves, gaining internal clarity that expands into external clarity.

Our world is a busy place, guided by a culture that thrives on multitasking. There are more prescription drugs than ever being used to deal with anxiety, stress, and depression. If we are scurrying from task to task and appointment to appointment, our minds will be cluttered, leaving little space for clarity or leadership.

One of the ways the most powerful leaders seek clarity is by taking time for themselves. They've learned that our personal habits are foundational to our broader corporate success. When we take time to nourish ourselves, we have greater capacity to see the big picture, allowing us to make wiser decisions and plan more effectively. I have certainly found this to be true. In fact, I am often asked how I have such a high capacity and still maintain clarity. Here are my "secrets":

Culture Infusion

- Indulge in natural vitamin D by doing a physical activity outdoors.

- Take time regularly for quiet meditation or mindfulness practices.

- Schedule a play date with family or friends.

- Breathe deeply when feeling stress or confusion.

- Smile.

- Stretch to release the tension you hold in your muscles.

- Listen to music daily.

- Eat healthy foods.

- Drink plenty of water.

- Get enough rest. Skimping on sleep and downtime is not a badge of honor. (Not convinced? Read Arianna Huffington's book *Thrive*.)

- Practice appreciation for everyone and everything (more on this in Principle 6).

- Listen as you engage with others (this includes putting down your cell phone or turning it off when interacting with others).

- Delegate and empower your team.

Follow Your Intuition

The final thing leaders do to round out their internal awareness? They listen to their intuition. In her book *Your 3 Best Super Powers*, Sonia Choquette defines intuition (one of the three superpowers) as "our natural GPS, our internal guide, our radar, our protection, our truth serum, our connector, our inner light, and the voice of our Higher Self."[7]

What is your gut telling you? What is your "leaning" on something you're questioning, or a decision you're trying to make? You might not be able to put it into words, but you probably have a feeling as to what's the right next move. Can you remember a time you did not follow your inner direction? How did it feel when you realized you should have followed your instincts?

A practice that I use is to check in with myself by asking, "Does it feel good?" Or, as those that know me ask, "What is the Kerry gut?" For example, I follow this practice on all our new hires. If my gut reaction is no for any reason, we will not move forward with the candidate. Years ago, I did not realize there was scientific evidence to support the validity of my "gut reaction" (the HeartMath Institute calls it your "heart reaction"[8]), but it turns out that approaching life from your heart center is better for you both physically and socially.

Yes, this is an effective strategy even in the business world! In *Your 3 Best Super Powers*, Choquette references two powerful examples. Bill Gates attributed much of his success with Microsoft to intuition, saying that to win big, "Often you have to rely on intuition." And Albert Einstein said, "The only real valuable thing is intuition," and came up with his Theory of Relativity via an intuitive dream.[9]

Pause to check in with what you know is the truth.

Malcolm Gladwell's book *Blink* discusses all aspects of making quick choices. Gladwell notes, "Improvisation comedy is a wonderful example of the kind of thinking that *Blink* is about. It involves people making very sophisticated decisions on the spur of the moment, without the benefit of any kind of script or plot."[10] Improvising in the moment is necessary for leaders in the thick of negotiations or when communicating in person, and it is an example of trusting and acting on your intuition on the spot versus thinking about how you are feeling.

Remember, though, that in order to tap into our intuition, we have to remove the static and get clear, intentionally tuning into our inner guidance through quiet self-reflection and awareness, as well as something else you might not expect: play.

During Sonia Choquette's three-part training on intuition activation, I learned that not only do I need to take time for self-reflection, I also must make time to play and enjoy life. I love spending time with my kids and teaching kid's yoga; they are my best teachers on tapping into my inner playful self. These play activities loosen anxiety, opening up the path to much clearer intuition. (We'll talk more about play in Principle 2: Prioritize Personal Wellness.)

Of course, a leader cannot succeed with an internal-only focus, so next let's also look at key areas of external focus.

Understand One Size Does Not Fit All

Successful leaders recognize that one size does not fit all. We wouldn't expect each of our children to have the same strengths and ways of communicating and working, would we? Then we shouldn't expect that of our employees. Exceptional leaders not only realize that each person on their team is a unique individual, but they also intentionally (there's that word again!) use those differences to the best advantage of each team member and the organization.

Successful leaders fully utilize the varying assets, personalities, and ages of their employees to facilitate individual and corporate well-being. The best leaders take time to disperse tasks and formulate teams to accurately play to each person's strengths.

Remember Generational Views Differ

One key component leaders need to contend with these days is the significant gap between people who were born in the information age and those who were born before it. These generations have vastly contrasting views on topics such as the type of working environment they prefer, what motivates them, their technological know-how, and how they set career goals.

For instance, according to the Center for Generational Kinetics, a company that is led by Traditionalists (born 1925–1945) and Baby Boomers (born 1946–1964) tends to use a command-and-control style of leadership set by strict rules. Traditionalists and Baby Boomers prefer a more formal working environment, are motivated by self-worth, believe in personal contact in interactions, and tend to have careers at one company or in one industry. On the other hand, Generations X (born 1965–1980) and Y (aka "Millennials," born 1981–2000) prefer a more casual working environment, are motivated by security as well as the ability to maintain work/life balance, were the first generations to be brought up with the use of technology, tend to work towards developing skills that are transferable, and can juggle parallel careers such as having a full-time job and freelancing or having another business on the side.[11]

Culture Infusion

This knowledge of what motivates each generation is helpful both in facilitating individual workplace satisfaction and in compiling high-functioning teams. Leaders who build intergenerational teams can use the wisdom and strong work ethics of Traditionalists and Baby Boomers to build the best operational practices and utilize the latest technology with the expertise of Generations X and Y.

My cousins in their twenties are good examples of Millennials who have a lack of satisfaction with their work. They frequently talk about work, particularly the frustrating parts of their jobs. One of my cousins is a women's clothing buyer, and after two years, she is the only one left of those who were on her team when she started. She was considering interviewing with a competitor, noting that the only reason to stay with her current employer is that she has more visibility as the only team member standing.

Another cousin works for a large consulting firm. For the past two years, he has been assigned to the same project because it has a high profit margin and he has mastered the project. Unfortunately, he is also extremely underutilized and bored at work. He is highly intelligent, and not being challenged is causing him significant stress. Meetings with his manager are just going out for lunch or drinks, not engaging in useful career discussions. Although he takes accountability for his career by telling his manager what he wants, the response is consistent: the project has high profit margins and the clients love him, so he remains on the same project. Unhappy and not using his full capacity, he is staying at his job now just to build up time with a large firm.

Another cousin is a financial analyst. After only a few months at his job, he feels he is just a number. He has had access to information on how the company releases employees, and he sees that employees who are high earners "will just get canned."

As I sat and listened to these stories, I was reminded how important it is for larger firms to take better care of their new talent and learn how to relate to those from other generations. Taking time to engage in conversation to ensure team members are heard and understood is much less costly than attrition caused by job dissatisfaction. Imagine the following:

- The women's clothing buyer gets called into her manager's office. She tells her how important she is and how much they want her to stay on the team. She asks her what she wants—perhaps it is more responsibility she is seeking—and they work towards offering steps to ensure her career is moving towards her aspirations. Simply taking time to ask and listen: win-win.

- The employee at the large consulting firm is given a new side project that ignites his intelligence and creativity. Win-win.

- The financial analyst is given a mentor. He learns the basics of the company as well as his role, and sees that he is valued and more secure at the company than he realized. Win-win.

As Simon Sinek discusses in an interview on the *Inside Quest* podcast, it is the "company's responsibility"[12] to form relationships of trust with Millennials. These employees need to be engaged. They need the two-way conversations with managers that ensure accountability of career aspirations from both sides. Otherwise, I envision my cousins—all highly talented employees—leaving to spread their wings, and their companies once again bearing the costs of attrition.

From a broader perspective, keeping employees happy with your firm gives you tenured employees, and having tenured employees gives your firm credibility. At Actualize, our internal operations team has been together since 2006. When we are interviewing new talent, sharing how the team that runs the operations of the firm has stayed together all these years inspires recruits and helps them gain confidence in a culture they want to be a part of.

Lead by Example

Another external aspect of leadership is the example that leaders set for their teams. The successful leaders are the ones who intentionally use their behavior as a positive example. If you expect employees to work overtime for important deadlines, for example, your team is much more inclined to do their best if you also stay and work the overtime, contributing to the success versus demotivating them and giving them reasons to blame you for their extra hours. Then when your team pulls through successfully, reward them well, either through recognition, time off, or monetary compensation. A simple message to the entire firm expressing your gratitude for a job well done can be a powerful tool that costs you nothing yet makes your team feel valued and important.

Our founding partner, Chad, is and always has been our most billable consultant at Actualize, so when he asks employees to go the extra mile, they respect his request. They know he is working harder than anyone while also leading by example to achieve exceptional client satisfaction.

Another lead-by-example scenario is about the action you do *not* take. Do not feed into office politics or gossip. As Eleanor Roosevelt emphasized in her book *You Learn by Living*, "Great minds discuss ideas; average minds discuss events; small minds discuss people."[13] If you hear your team talking negatively about someone or something, bring up a point that is positive about that person or event to turn the focus around. Remind your team that each challenging person or situation allows us an opportunity to grow. Show your team that you can rise above and maintain a level of both professionalism and gratitude. Your positive attitude benefits everyone.

No matter your level in the firm, your actions will be followed. If you are nice to someone, they will respond kindly; if you act with compassion, others will treat you with compassion; if you are engaged, others will follow your lead; if you smile at someone, they will smile back at you. Use teamwork towards a common goal, and you reinforce the fact that you are indeed all on the same team.

Bring Your Heart to Work

When it all comes down to it, as a leader the most solid foundation on which you can build is your heart. Leading from the heart is looking at each situation through compassion and kindness and having empathy for each team member. When you lead from your heart, you will get to know your team (whether they report to you or not) and their unique skills and insights. You will show you care in all your interactions, even the difficult ones. You will lead by example, with a positive attitude that others will agree to follow, even when they're not 100 percent on board.

Leaders such as Eleanor Roosevelt, Martin Luther King Jr., Mother Teresa, and Thomas Jefferson each led from their heart. They were not worried about what others might think because they believed their focus on others' rights and feelings was most important. To lead, you must allow yourself to make decisions based on how you feel and take into consideration the impact your decisions might have on your employees. We have found focusing on culture instead of profit actually leads to improved growth and profit through a more engaged and happy employee base.

> **When you lead from the heart, you will, in essence, be building a corporate culture based on the greatest renewable resource of all: love.**

There is even scientific data to support the value of an open heart. In his book *Joy on Demand: The Art of Discovering the Happiness Within*, Chade-Meng Tan gives the following easy-to-understand explanation around the physical brain-heart connection, or "neurocardiac coupling": "In a state of kindness or compassion, for example, your vagus nerve gets activated. One thing that does is it relaxes the muscles around the heart, so you experience the physical sensation of 'opening of the heart.'" Tan goes on to describe, "Somehow, we know to trust people with strong vagal tone."[14] Which clarifies why complete strangers will tell me what is going on with them at a personal level and then say, "Wow, I have no idea why I told you that!"

According to the Institute of HeartMath, there is an actual electromagnetic energy involved here:

> The human heart emits the strongest electromagnetic field in our body. The heart's electromagnetic field is five thousand times stronger than the brain's electromagnetic field. This electromagnetic field envelops the entire body extending out in all directions, and it can be measured up to several feet outside of the body. Research shows that as we consciously focus on feeling a positive emotion it has a beneficial effect on our own health and well-being, and can have a positive affect [sic] on those around us.[15]

Apparently, my practices to open my heart both emotionally (self-reflection) and physically (movement and play) are having a positive impact on those around me. You, too, can have a similar impact on yourself and others by leading from the heart and practicing overall personal wellness as I discuss in Principle 2: Prioritize Personal Wellness.

Conclusion

Although every person is different, we universally do well with leaders who focus on appreciation, respect, and trust, and who empower teams to add value to the company. Exceptional leaders know the best ways to motivate employees, retain quality talent, and cultivate job satisfaction.

Internal and external insights provide input to make these informed leadership decisions. For instance, taking time to ensure our employees are aligning goals to their strengths will pay off in the long run. Hounding an employee to focus on something they do not enjoy is not motivating and does nothing to help job satisfaction.

For example, many years ago, I realized that I was an extreme micromanager and also had a hard time delegating work. I was so busy trying to finish all my work and watch over every little aspect of other people's work that I wasn't able to focus on developing strategic vision. When I finally realized something needed to change, I took my internal tasks and divided them amongst my team according to each of our strengths, specifically allowing alignment towards our best attributes. As a result, we now all have more job satisfaction and dedication to the team and the work. I regularly check in with how they are doing, but now rather than pushing them I ask genuinely how I can help them be successful and stay motivated and inspired. Even though I know I will never be perfect, I am constantly working to improve as a leader so I can support my team.

In conclusion, leaders can infuse intentional leadership into their organization in these areas:

- Focus first on their personal well-being
- Practice self-awareness and reflection
- Set and follow intentions
- Create clarity for themselves and their organization
- Hone and follow their intuition
- Leverage the team members' diversity
- Lead by example
- Bring their heart to work

MIND-EXPANDING EXPERIENCES

Personal

Ask yourself the following questions: "How do I handle feedback? Am I able to calmly process the information and take forward action steps, or do I become defensive?" Go back to a time when you were defensive when you were given feedback. Write down how you could have made better choices in forward action steps.

Team

Have your team use the following questions to reflect on leaders that have inspired them over the years. Different qualities will stand out for each of us, helping us determine what resonates with us in regards to leadership.

1. Who do you think of as pivotal leaders from the past?
2. What current leaders stand out to you?
3. What qualities do these leaders have?
4. Who has been most influential to you as a leader in your career? Why?
5. How can the leadership of our firm mirror these same qualities? Provide 2–4 suggestions.

After this exercise, work to implement the suggestions into the culture of your organization.

Culture Infusion

Practice setting and following intentions with your organization. What are two intentions for your organization as a whole that you would like to progress on in the next six months? How will you communicate and measure success of those intentions? In your opinion, what results would portray a successful outcome?

PRINCIPLE 2

Prioritize Personal Wellness

Energy out <—> Energy in

Successful leaders prioritize personal wellness, both at home and at work. Successful organizations follow that lead by integrating work/life balance into their organizational culture. For instance, if team members see their leadership team focusing on personal well-being by taking time off to go to their child's school play, using their lunch break to move, utilizing breathing exercises as they are handling challenging situations, and interacting in playful ways, others will be more inclined to follow their lead.

In one of my favorite business books, *The Power of Full Engagement* by Jim Loehr and Tony Schwartz, the second principle states, "Because energy capacity diminishes both with overuse and underuse, we must balance expenditure with intermittent energy renewal."[16] In other words, we need to remember that energy is a two-way street. And in *Your Brain at Work*, David Rock says that "switching between tasks uses energy; if you do this a lot you can make more mistakes."[17]

So how do we keep our energy in balance? How do we remember to pay attention to our energy fluctuations? With intentional daily practices, which, when done often enough, with enough consistency, become welcome routines.

This section will discuss several energy-balancing practices that do not require specialized skills, just...well...practice.

Guiding Values

When I was traveling more for my job and taking on more special projects, my daughter's class needed a room mom and someone to lead the monthly art program. Since nobody else volunteered to help, I agreed to take on both roles, not knowing how I would handle it all with my new work schedule.

What I did know was that I absolutely needed to prioritize my self-care, embedding it into my daily routine and getting up earlier to take care of myself. In fact, I needed to *amplify* my self-care routine, committing to take care of myself first and foremost. Many mothers find this idea conflicts with their care-for-others-first nature, but I can assure you that self-care is not selfish! I have fewer moments of anger and frustration when I prioritize me time, whereas before I was resentful because I was not taking time for activities that I love and that light me up. I am now taking accountability for my happiness versus being resentful of those I care for.

Even though I was busy, I knew I must not skimp on quiet time or moving my body. Quiet time gives me the emotional and brain space I need for clarity, so I made that time a non-negotiable requirement for myself. On the days I did not have much time for movement, I had to get creative, turning to singing and dancing. Maybe I couldn't go for a walk or run that day, but I could always make time to sing and dance to at least one song (although I typically do more than that). It is a fun, fast, effective way to move and lift your vibration. My teacher Sonia Choquette offers a great example of this, having us dance and sing and play each time we meet for classes!

At the end of that school year, I felt better than ever regarding work, my kids, and my overall well-being. I learned that if I make time for myself, I actually am more engaged and have more capacity in all areas of my life.

Through much trial and error, I have landed on five guiding values for personal wellness that help me stay well in all areas of my life:

1. Breathe

2. Move

3. Play

4. Nourish

5. Replenish

In this chapter, I will walk you through these five simple yet powerful guiding values and how you can use them daily as your path to ongoing wellness. In addition to the Mind-Expanding Experiences section at the end of the chapter, within the chapter I share other exercises and practices.

Breathe

The truth is that many of us forget to breathe during the day. Yes, we breathe enough to stay alive, but we don't breathe in ways that take full advantage of the powerful ally our breath can be.

We are going to have emotional ups and downs throughout any day, going from being happy to angry or sad and back again. We are going to get stuck in traffic jams. We will have people we love pass away—as I was compiling this book, my childhood best friend passed away. In these times of stress, we can turn to our breath. It is free, accessible to us at any time, and a powerful antidote to anxiety and the physical symptoms of stress.

An article from Harvard Medical School notes that one healthy way to handle stress is through the "relaxation response," a term coined by Dr. Herbert Benson,[18] cardiologist and founder of the Benson-Henry Institute for Mind Body Medicine at Massachusetts General Hospital. Following is an excerpt from the article "Relaxation Techniques: Breath Control Helps Quell Errant Stress Response": "The relaxation response is a state of profound rest that can be elicited in many ways, including meditation, yoga, and progressive muscle relaxation...Breath focus is a common feature of several techniques that evoke the relaxation response. The first step is learning to breathe deeply."[19]

EXERCISE: BREATHING ATTENTION

Stop for a moment and notice your breathing. Ask yourself the following questions:

1. Am I holding my breath, or breathing freely?

2. Am I taking deep or shallow breaths?

3. Do my throat, chest, and abdomen feel tight or relaxed?

If you don't think your breathing is affected during the day, try the following exercise:

1. Set an alarm to alert you once per hour for each hour you are awake.

2. Each time the alarm rings, notice your breathing.

3. Ask yourself questions 1–3 above.

4. Practice a few minutes of breathing. You can simply breathe or use your favorite breathing app (such as Breathe2Relax, GPS for the Soul, or, if you have an Apple Watch, the Breathe app).

Chances are that many times when the alarm goes off you will either be restricting your breath or actually holding your breath. I now know that sometimes I hold my breath simply because I'm concentrating on what I'm doing!

Culture Infusion

The good news is that simply focusing on taking a few long, slow breaths can bring you back to the present moment and help calm you down. My teacher Rolf Gates told me an old Japanese fable about this: A man gets hit by a car. Because it was his practice to breathe ten times before any reaction, after getting hit by the car he took ten breaths, smiled, and walked away.

The next time you find yourself stressed, upset at a co-worker, about to scream, and wanting to hide under your desk or just go home sick, take a moment to breathe. Focus on a deep inhale and a slow exhale. There are many complicated breathing techniques you could use, yet just having an awareness of your breath and taking a few mindful breaths will even out your energy in any situation. And remember the fable of the Japanese man; it will put a smile on your face. Anytime my emotions start to go negative, I will simply use one of my breathing techniques (I try my best to practice what I teach).

Simple, Fun Breathing Prompts

To remind people to practice wellness, I have created fun, squeezable cubes for different themes, with a different prompt on each side. I keep one on my desk as a reminder and throughout the day will do one of the exercises to pause. Try these prompts from the Breathing cube throughout your day:

- **Belly breathing:** Inhale slowly through your nose, pretending to blow up a balloon in your belly. Wait two seconds, then slowly exhale through your mouth, emptying the balloon of air so your tummy deflates.

- **Balloon breathing:** Raise your arms from your sides up over your head as you take a deep breath. As you exhale, let all the air come out like a balloon as you drop your arms.

- **Ahhhh:** Take a long breath in and say, "Ahhhh."

- **Hummm:** Start to hum, then place your hands over your ears. Notice how the sound changes. Continue to move your hands on and off your ears.

- **Breathing:** Smile, hum, say "ahhhh," blow your belly up with air, and breathe.

As you can see, these breathing exercises don't require a lot of time or energy. They *do*, however, require attention, so practice bringing awareness to your breath each day. (The cubes can be found at http://www.zendoway.com/cubes.html.)

Move

Movement is another way of taking care of your own well-being. You may be expecting me to send you to a gym or a track to do a hard workout, but that's not what I'm talking about here. This section is about gentler physical movement that you can engage in several times during the day as a way to keep your body and mind more relaxed and energized.

I learned in my yoga training that opposites heal. Many of the aches and pains we experience are due to us not moving our bodies. Many of us are sedentary most of the day, sitting at desks then lounging at home in the evening. We are not made to sit like this all day every day; we need to do the opposite of sitting and *move!* If, for example, you sit for hours typing, take regular short breaks to counter the typing motion with some simple stretches of your hands and wrists. To counter your sitting position, simply stand up and walk around your chair every hour.

Taking time to move your body during the day helps to keep you focused and fresh. As my teacher Rolf Gates says in *Meditations from the Mat*, "We must see that our movements, like the quieting of the mind, have the potential to access an intelligence that has not been available to us. Connection to this intelligence, the wisdom of evolution, will gradually deepen as we cultivate it day after day in our practice."[20] Moving creates space for "creative expression," as Gates would say in his classes.

EXERCISES: SIMPLE MOVEMENTS

The following simple exercises can be done at your desk throughout the day. *The key is to perform these movements mindfully and frequently. Hold each position for 2–3 breaths.*

- **Circles:** Slowly move your wrists and ankles in circles, alternating between rotating them and flexing them. Shake your hands and arms lightly. Cautiously move your neck slowly from right to left.

- **Massage:** One body part we easily miss is our ears, yet an ear massage offers great benefits. The Chinese have used ear reflexology for thousands of years to address many types of health issues in the body. By simply rubbing, pulling, and gently twisting your ears, you stimulate energy points that run through your body, creating a sense of renewal and relaxation.

Try this now. Then take a few minutes to massage your hands, forearms, and neck.

- **Stretching:** While at your desk, clasp your hands and raise them above your head, reaching tall. Holding the tall reach, move your extended hands, arms, and upper body smoothly and slowly from side to side.

- **Poses:** Yes, you can do yoga poses at your desk and around the office without drawing much attention. (Although I have heard of co-workers doing headstands and walking on their hands in the office, I am not suggesting that!) Who knows, your co-workers might even join you.

  - *Child's Pose:* Sitting in a chair, slowly lean forward and fold your head over your knees while relaxing the back of your neck. Clasp your hands behind your legs or dangle them lightly by your sides.

  - *Cat/Cow:* Sit with your hands on your knees and place your feet on the floor. Inhale while you arch your back and look upwards, then exhale while you round your spine and let your head drop gently forward.

  - *Seated Spinal Twist:* Sit up tall in your chair. Put your hands on either the back of your chair or the arm rest. Twist gently and hold for a few seconds. Repeat with the other side.

- **Hip Stretch:** Sitting in your chair, place your right foot on the floor directly under your right knee. Place your left ankle over your right knee and flex your foot (toes towards knee). Inhale while you sit up tall to lengthen your lower back. Exhale while you lean slightly forward, feeling a stretch in your left hip. Repeat on the other side.

- **Walking:** Make an effort to get up from your desk each hour, even if just for a bathroom or water break. Take that "up" time to focus on deep breathing and mindfully walking and stretching.

Note: Visit http://www.zendoway.com/relaxation-videos.html for a series of four- to five-minute routines you can do at your desk.

One particularly fun movement is dance, made even more fun by adding singing. Each day, take time to sing a song in the car while "car dancing," or dance and sing before you go to work or while you're doing housework. If you are upset or angry, instead of stewing over it, dance or sing it out. You can go back to being upset if you must, but often you will simply let it go and stay with your better mood. Give it a try and see how you feel.

Play

One thing many of us forget to do as adults is to play. Think of a time you remember playing as a kid. What were you doing? How did it feel? When was the last time you played? Take time daily to frolic, be silly, or play a game of cards or I Wonder with someone (the options are nearly endless!).

Playing is contagious. If we choose to be playful, it is hard for those around us not to engage. This is perfectly illustrated by the polar bear and the dog in Stuart Brown's TED Talk "Play Is More Than Just Fun."[21] Brown shows the audience a picture of a wild polar bear ready to fight a tethered dog. But instead of having the dog as a meal, he says, the polar bear began to play with her. Why? Because the dog was in a play stance, so the polar bear simply joined in.

Play isn't *only* fun and games, though. Did you know there is actually a science-based organization called the National Institute for Play? Their work "unlocks the human potential through play in all stages of life using science to discover all that play has to teach us about transforming our world." The National Institute for Play notes that while current research points to the benefits of play, there are still gaps in the data, which the Institute is working to fill:

> A huge amount of existing scientific research—from neurophysiology, developmental and cognitive psychology, to animal play behavior, and evolutionary and molecular biology—contains rich data on play. The existing research describes patterns and states of play and explains how play shapes our brains, creates our competencies, and ballasts our emotions. The research from these diverse areas of science must be integrated to depict human play mechanisms as a whole. The

integration work will reveal critical gaps where additional basic research is required.[22]

If play is something important enough to dedicate research resources to, I think that's a good reason for each of us to keep play in our daily lives. Let's keep an eye on the Institute's findings!

Play is also important because it engages the imagination. In her book *Your 3 Best Super Powers*, Sonia Choquette identifies imagination as one of the three superpowers we all have. Play is not an optional component of success—it is essential!

Next time you find yourself stressing, trying hard to figure something out, give your brain a break and call your inner child out for a play date. I had a client trying to find a way to encourage play with full-time employees and subcontractors together—while not violating any legal rules of treating subcontractors like employees—so I suggested a Lunch and Play where they have mini tournaments with games such as Jenga, Chinese Checkers, or Connect Four over lunch.

> **"Play doesn't just help us to explore what is essential. It is essential in and of itself."**
>
> **—Greg McKeown**

Daniel H. Pink's book *A Whole New Mind* has an entire section devoted to play. One activity Pink suggests is adding captions to cartoons. The *New Yorker* magazine has a contest every month or you can simply cut the captions off and enlist some friends or co-workers to come up with your own captions. Pink also suggests taking a humor test to determine how you cope. The research from this test denotes that "those who score high on a multidimensional sense of humor scale have lower levels of depression and higher levels of purpose than those who score low in humor."[23] Pink also suggests play through inventing, playing online games, going back to school, dissecting a joke, and playing right-brain games.

Nourish

Although you might not think of nourishment as an important ingredient of a healthy culture, food is a big part of our lives, and what we eat does affect our personal wellness, which in turn impacts the culture. Yes, we eat to fill our body, but do we intentionally eat in a way that gives us positive energy? In this section, I use the term "nourish" to refer to much more than just putting food into our bodies. It's about taking the time to get to know our own nutrition needs, and to lovingly provide for those needs in a way that is life-giving and positive.

If we are not eating a well-balanced diet, our personal performance, whether at home or at work, can be negatively impacted. Think about the days you had a coffee and a chocolate bar (or a treat from the loved/hated box of donuts in the break room) to get you over that afternoon slump. I'm guessing it did the trick for about fifteen minutes, and then your energy faded out, likely to even lower than before. That is not a healthy way to nourish yourself. This section offers you other ways to not just boost your energy but to maintain a consistent energy level so you can work without fighting sleep or a foggy or totally wired brain.

I learned the importance of balanced nourishment the hard way. I have struggled with food my entire life; I was the girl at sleepovers in high school who didn't get to eat the junk food because I was always watching my weight. I learned at a young age that I have a slow metabolism, yet I love food and sweets. Those two situations do not mix well, so for years I tried the only solution I knew of: significant food restrictions. I was miserable.

It has taken me years to realize that depriving ourselves is a losing battle because we just want what we can't have. Instead, *moderation* and *balance* are the key words and actions. We really need to "feel" food out, trying different amounts, types, and combinations of foods that taste good *and* make us feel good. I get so worked up when I hear about the latest diets and this, that, and the other "trick" to make it easier to deprive yourself of food. *Please do not just follow the diet hype.* You have to do what is right for *you* and is going to work for *your* lifestyle and *your* food preferences.

Maybe you are a vegetarian, or just don't eat red meat, or maybe you are all about the red meat, or can't stand the taste of dairy. Any of those preferences is *fine!* The key is to ensure that you have a balanced mix of the food groups, always including plenty of fruits and vegetables. Perhaps the easiest way to think about positive nourishment is as eating more foods that come from nature, rather than processed foods.

Below is a list of simple daily nourishment habits to keep you feeling energized and strong:

- **Start your day with a cup of warm lemon water** to refresh your system. Yes, you can still have your coffee or tea afterwards; just give your body a little cleanse first thing. Would you put bad fuel in your car and go on a long road trip? No. You always follow instructions to ensure your car is running at its best because it gets you around from place to place. Treat your body at least that well.

- **Drink water throughout the day.** Our bodies are made up of approximately 70 percent water, so we must continue to provide a healthy supply to keep our bodies happy. Next time you reach for a snack, try this age-old trick: drink a glass of water instead. Why? Because often you are thirsty, not hungry. If you miss the appeal of a snack, try putting some lemon or other fruit in your water to give it some flavor.

- **Keep only healthy snacks at home and in the office.** I know this is a basic tip, but we can all use the reminder. If you are hungry and don't have something healthy to eat close by, you will most likely grab the cake or cookies in the pantry. The analogy I teach my kids is, "Would you feed your dog a bowl of sugar?"

- **Cut up fruit and vegetables** to have on hand at all times. Even if you don't love fruits and vegetables, after a short time this habit will grow on you and you'll realize how flavorful and satisfying they are. Really!

- **Eat whole foods and healthy fats** to ensure you are satisfied throughout the day. When you focus on eating whole foods, the processed sugary foods are limited and you feel more sustained throughout the day.

Again, do what works for you, and be mindful of your body and the fuel you put into your system. The healthier choices you make, the better you will feel, and the more energy you will have to be the best at all you do on a daily basis.

Replenish

Deepak Chopra often says, "Meditation is not a way of making your mind quiet. It's a way of entering into the quiet that's already there—buried under the 50,000 thoughts the average person thinks every day." In our busy, production-oriented society, we don't often stop to push the noise of regular life to the side, but taking quiet time to replenish yourself is probably something you can use more of. Some call this reflection, introspection, meditation, or something else, but let's keep it simple and call it "quiet time."

Taking time to simply be quiet, in a quiet environment, is an important daily practice. This is a way to give yourself a break from the outside world and focus for a few minutes on your heart and soul. Your mind will try to run the show and get you up and checking off your to-do list, but with practice, your thoughts will fade out and you will just hear silence. Your mind will quickly begin to settle from the constant distractions and responsibilities.

If you're thinking, *I'm too busy to do this!* quiet time might be exactly what you need. When we least feel we can afford to take time away from our crazy busy schedule, that's when we most need a break. I know that's true because for a long time, my energy was definitely unbalanced towards depletion. I was carrying out Einstein's definition of insanity, doing the same thing over and over and expecting different results. Trying harder and getting more worn out and frustrated. I finally slowed down and started taking regular quiet time to myself when I turned my on again, off again yoga practice into a daily practice.

I am an avid runner, and found that yoga helped loosen my consistently tight hamstrings. Even just a few minutes each day made me a better athlete and a healthier person. When I finally slowed down and began taking regular quiet time for myself, it wasn't long until l felt my energy building again. I was moving from thinking to feeling and was driven to explore more of the "good" feelings of tapping into the present moment. And during challenging situations, it allows me to access that sense of calm in dealing with others (or at least trying my best, as it does take practice to not react).

If you are new to this practice, one way to quiet your mind is to write down things you are grateful for or things you wish to come true. Or if you have an issue you are dealing with, consider writing a letter to the person or about the issue (whether you plan to send it or not). Try your best not to judge yourself; just write honestly. Writing can often help you come to a better understanding of what is going on or to focus on the positive when you're finding life overwhelming.

> "An integral being knows without going, sees without looking, and accomplishes without doing."
>
> —Lao Tzu

As time progresses, you might want to use this quiet time to do nothing. What you do—or don't do—during your quiet time is up to you. Notice what feels like it will renew your energy on any given day, and choose that, making sure that it is something that allows you to feel quiet inside.

Culture Infusion

Quiet time is so important because it gives us a chance to listen to our heart, to get a feeling about something instead of just trying to think through it. Our bodies hold a lot of wisdom, and when we begin to pay regular attention to them, our intuition strengthens. A tight chest might mean a tight heart wanting to be more open. A knotted stomach when you think of one option and a relaxed stomach when you think of another might lead you to your best choice in a situation. If your throat is constricted, maybe you need to speak out about something or express yourself in a situation you're dealing with. With practice, you will start learning how to read your body signals.

My best ideas come from my quiet time. I am sure that is why many of the great pioneers, artists, and scientists spent hours of each day walking and contemplating. Beethoven used to work from dawn to mid-afternoon, taking many breaks for walks to encourage his creativity. Psychotherapist Carl Jung, philosopher Søren Kierkegaard, composer Franz Schubert, authors Victor Hugo and Charles Dickens, and many others considered walks essential to their creative and productive routines. Walking is also a great excuse to spend time in and with nature. Henry David Thoreau's *Walking* is famous for its discussion on nature. In the first sentence of this essay, Thoreau notes the "absolute freedom and wildness" of nature: "I wish to speak a word for Nature, for absolute freedom and wildness, as contrasted with a freedom and culture merely civil, —to regard man as an inhabitant, or a part and parcel of Nature, rather than a member of society." The essay continues, discussing key points about being in nature and what one can learn from that experience.[24]

I find that anything in nature will immediately calm my entire body. For you, maybe it's watching a sunset, spending time with your dog or cat, or just taking a walk outside and looking around you. Movement and play can be even more enjoyable if practiced outside.

Studies show a variety of benefits from time in nature. According to an article by the Ecosystem Services Team of the U.S. Department of Agriculture, the Forest Service, and Pacific Northwest Research Station:

> "Parks and other natural environments are a fundamental health resource, particularly in terms of disease prevention" (Maller et al. 2008). Researchers are demonstrating the positive effects of nature on blood pressure, cholesterol, outlook on life, and stress reduction. It has also proven beneficial to those with attention deficit disorder (Kuo and Taylor 2004). Spending time in nature also has been linked to longevity and decreased risk of mental illness in studies in Scandinavia and the Netherlands (De Vries et al. 2003, Grahn and Stigsdotter 2003).[25]

GETTING BACK TO NATURE

Think back to your favorite memories with nature. For each memory, answer the following questions:

1. Where were you?

2. What do you remember most clearly?

3. What did you do to feel a sense of peace or play?

4. How can you re-create that feeling in your current life?

Take one of your answers to the last question and schedule time on your calendar to do just that.

If you are concerned that taking quiet time is helpful for your personal life but conflicts with a productive corporate culture, I'll just mention that Google has an entire employee training program on meditation. Also, I've already mentioned one of Google's pioneers, Chade-Meng Tan, who wrote a *New York Times* bestseller called *Search Inside Yourself*, focusing on meditation and how to incorporate it into the workplace. (You will find more about this in Principle 6: Focus on Your People.)

You may be surprised at what you uncover and the ideas you have when you take a little time to settle your mind and listen to your heart. You deserve to be the best you can be, so try daily quiet time for a few weeks and notice the difference.

Conclusion

As you consider your own personal well-being, it is important to remember that *you* create your life and how you feel. Change starts at the individual level.

Take time to nurture and care for yourself from the center of your own heart. As Vietnamese Buddhist monk, teacher, author, poet, and peace activist Thich Nhat Hanh frequently says, "smile, breathe, and go slowly." Then trust yourself and the gut feelings of your intuition. If it does not *feel* right, chances are it is not right. As Sonia Choquette says in her classes, "Nobody has ever come back to me saying, 'I trusted my true spirit and it was wrong.'"

Finally, remember to follow the Guiding Values for Personal Wellness:

1. Breathe
2. Move
3. Play
4. Nourish
5. Replenish

MIND-EXPANDING EXPERIENCES

Personal

First, take a moment to reflect on how often you take time for yourself. Next, identify what activities bring you to your natural peaceful state. Make a list of ways you nurture yourself and what brings you joy.

To make change stick, I ask you to commit to taking time for yourself for thirty days. Record in your journal what you do each day and the impacts you noticed. Better yet, enlist the support of a loved one to join you and keep each other accountable for a daily dose of nurturing.

Team

Because we are sitting the majority of the day, most team members will appreciate a moment to move. Consider beginning your next meeting with the stretching exercise mentioned earlier:

1. Have everyone stand up.
2. Next, ask them to clasp their hands and raise them above their head, reaching tall.
3. Holding the tall reach, move their extended hands, arms, and upper body smoothly and slowly from side to side.

Another fun, easy way to start a meeting is to play a song that everyone knows the words too. Simply have them sit and sing, or ask them to stand up and dance.

Culture Infusion

Consider implementing programs to incorporate the Guiding Values into your firm's operations. For instance:

- Start meetings with movement, breathing, play, or dance.

- Encourage team members to conduct walking meetings when appropriate.

- Offer opportunities for teams to play in and out of the office.

- Provide healthy food options at work.

- Facilitate breathing and replenishment education and experiences.

These are just a few suggestions; there are endless possibilities. Focus on what would work for your firm.

PRINCIPLE 3

Insist on a Healthy Work/Life Balance

In addition to self-awareness, imagination, and conscience, it is the fourth human endowment—independent will—that really makes effective self-management possible...If you are an effective manager of yourself, your discipline comes from within; it is a function of your independent will.

—Stephen R. Covey, *The 7 Habits of Highly Effective People*

Work and home used to have much clearer boundaries than we now have in this information age of 24/7 connectivity. Work is often just a click away while at home, or at a kid's ballgame, or even a funeral or wedding, weekend, weekday, morning, or night. As the boundaries between work and home fade, leaders of successful organizations realize that it is up to them to model a healthy work/life balance and to facilitate the same in their teams.

We tend to blend work with just about everything else, but then compartmentalize how we *view* work versus our personal life and outside activities. We forget to compare the amount of time and energy we spend on each, which then quickly creates an imbalance between work and "other." In order to be the best you can be in all areas, *all* aspects of your life need to be in near balance. If you are working too much, then you will not have the energy to do things when you are not at work. If you play too hard outside of work, then you will not have the capacity you need to perform at your job.

Practicing your own work/life balance, then helping your company facilitate this work/life balance, will benefit you and your employees. They will be happier, healthier, and more motivated as they follow your example and see how much you care about their well-being.

A Word on Balance

Balance is a tricky thing. In fact, I'm not even sure absolute balance is possible at any given time. What is possible, however, is a balance *on average, over time.* Our lives are not steady and work is constantly changing, so the reality is that some days will require you to focus more on work, and other days more on personal life, tipping you off-balance. The key is to counterbalance your activities in order to bring your energy and focus closer to center.

If, for example, you worked late three nights in a row in order to finish a project, make sure you then plan extra time for play, rest, and time with people who energize and nourish you. Finish the week out being able to say you had, on average, a balanced week.

How to Achieve Work/Life Balance

As you know, a healthy work/life balance doesn't just happen. It is an ongoing series of tweaks and changes to what we focus on and participate in. Although those changes will look different for everyone, the following examples from my own life show the kinds of things we need to consider.

Say No

I was asked to work on a project that was throwing off my work/life balance and causing me stress because I was constantly thinking and worrying about the work. One day my nine-year-old daughter came to me and said, "Mom, you have never been this stressed out about work. Maybe you should reconsider." That comment made me realize things had to change, so after I fulfilled my initial contractual duties, I decided to step down from the project. There was potential to stay on further, but that would not have been healthy for me, as my own daughter had pointed out!

Fortunately, Actualize leadership agreed 100 **percent** with my decision. My brother had felt the project was taking me away from the core of Actualize work anyway, so that—plus me choosing a responsible time to leave the project—made it acceptable to leave. I had to take responsibility for myself, while considering the appropriate way to do that. If you find yourself in a situation where management does not agree with your saying no, determine if there are tasks you can delegate or ways you can be creative with your time.

There are plenty of times when I have had to just do what needed to be done. For example, I did not take maternity leave for either of my kids' births because we were in startup mode for

Actualize. Now my kids come first, and the lesson I learned is that when my work is impacting my role as a mother and how I interact with my kids, I have to make tough choices. What is best for me is going to flow down into all aspects of my life. I learned that standing up for my sanity is important for me *and* my family.

Set Boundaries

Protecting our employees' boundaries will instill a sense of trust. For example, striving to conduct interactions only during business hours is respectful of our team. Yes, there will be times when we ask for overtime or after-hours work, but it is important to be clear that it is not the norm. Additionally, if a team member is taking time off to be with family or go to an event, do your best to avoid contacting them via phone or email to ensure they have space to enjoy their time off.

In order to keep a reasonable work/life balance, I have also had to set and keep clear boundaries. For example, I used to take work calls from my brother late in the evening, and because I like to complete tasks as they come in, after these late calls I would stay up even later to finish the resulting tasks. Realizing how much this affected my own time, I finally requested that we not have any calls after 9 pm. That might seem late for some of you, but given that my brother works at all hours, 9 pm was a healthy boundary for me. We have managed to find other times for briefing and debriefing each other about work that meet both of our needs.

Handle Issues Now

Another important way to keep your work/life balance healthy is to handle issues as they come up instead of letting them simmer and take up important energy and space in your head.

If, for example, I have a disagreement with a co-worker and don't address it directly with that person, chances are that I will take that frustration home and keep thinking about it. Even though I'm home, my attention is still at work. Because I want to be able to be fully present where I am in the moment, I try my best to confront things as they come up rather than stewing over them.

At Actualize, leadership sets the tone with how we discuss things, always looking for a way to resolve an issue rather than blaming others and going through that cycle. We aim to face issues head on and, if necessary, bring all the impacted parties together for an open discussion. In fact, we created a process called the 3P Method to handle these situations. We pause to listen to each other (and understand), then pivot to the positive. (I discuss this in greater detail in Principle 5: Handle Conflict Directly, Openly, and Immediately.)

Moving forward in this way truly saves so much time. When you handle issues now, you keep them from spilling over much more than they need to.

Work Remotely

Another key factor of work/life balance is the ability to choose your work environment. While not all companies are on board, many fortunately do allow employees to work remotely, connected to the main office through technology, with little or no requirement to be physically in an office together.

Actualize is one of those companies. We are very focused on facilitating flexible schedules and allowing our employees to work from home if possible for internal and client work. In fact, my internal team has been remote for the entire span of Actualize's existence! I work out of my house and go into the office for meetings as necessary. My staff is not local to my area, and as working moms they greatly appreciate the location flexibility. I tell them that I don't mind if they go to their kids' school to volunteer for a few hours during the day as long as they get the job done and have coverage. I feel this is a big part of why my team is so loyal and so successful.

Continuing with the idea of boundaries introduced earlier, working from home is another area in which boundaries could turn gray. For my first eleven years at Actualize, I would get online around 6 am. In my twelfth year with the company, I started doing my personal movement and replenishment practices during that time, creating a boundary and allowing me to prioritize my personal well-being. Other options to consider are setting times when you will turn off your computer and sticking to working only during normal business hours. Otherwise, you will be drained by a sense of always being online and "at work," like I often am if I'm not careful.

In recent years we have also seen a significant shift in our clients' need for us to be on-site versus working remotely. With the use of technology such as GoToMeeting, Skype, Zoom, messaging apps, Dropbox, and other cloud technologies, as well as smartphones and email, we can do much more of our work off-site with no negative impact to our clients. That being said, typically at the beginning of a new engagement we have to be on-site to cultivate the in-person relationships. (Never underestimate the power of in-person interaction.)

It goes back to the word *balance*. Balance is obtained by easing into remote working. If possible for the work you do, and within company policy, commit to working from home at least one day a week, or even more if feasible. Encourage your staff to do so as well. If working from home is not currently an option in your organization, see if it *could* work on some level. Implement incrementally first by allowing a few hours, then one day a week. If working from home won't work, try allowing folks to work longer hours and take one day off each week. Get creative and your employees will see your heart shine through and know you really do care about their well-being.

If increases in performance, job satisfaction, and tenure aren't strong enough reasons for organizations to offer the work-from-home option, maybe pointing out the resulting improvement in work/life balance will tip the scales. It has definitely been a huge part of my ongoing satisfaction and commitment to my company.

Conclusion

I know it's easy to get caught up in all the things we need to get done each day. It might seem like having to pay attention to your work/life balance is just one more thing to add to the list, but I promise you it is worth adding. When your life is well balanced, on average, between work and other activities, you will be more satisfied, more motivated, happier, and healthier.

As Greg McKeown says in his book *Essentialism*, we have the option of "living by design, not default."[26] We have the power to choose what we engage in each day. We can take the initiative to design our life instead of having our life design us. We can choose balance.

Follow these practices to create work/life balance, on average, over time:

74

- Say no

- Set boundaries

- Handle issues now

- Work remotely (as feasible and if possible)

MIND-EXPANDING EXPERIENCES

Personal (Energy Assessment)

Awareness is an important part of managing a healthy work/life balance. Your schedule likely gives you a good idea of how much time you spend on work versus other activities, but do you know how much *energy* you spend? The following exercise will help you take an "energetic read" of your days.

Schedule ten minutes at the end of each day to do this exercise. It can be either your last task at work or before you go to bed. Try putting this daily practice on your calendar. Know you will not always complete it, yet the more you check in, the better your choices.

1. At the end of each day, find a quiet, comfortable place to sit and have a notebook and pen/pencil handy.

2. Take three long, deep breaths in and out to quiet your mind.

3. Turn your attention to your body and consider the following questions, recording your answers in your notebook:

- How does my body feel? (Relaxed? Tight? Something else?)

- On a scale of 1–10 (1 being lowest, 10 highest), how much positive energy do I have?

4. Now think back through the activities of the day and answer the following questions in your notebook. Don't take much time—just go with your gut-level reaction:

    - Based on my current energy, what activities—work or other—do I wish I had done more of (if any)? Less of?

BONUS:

At the end of the week, answer this question: Based on what I discovered from this exercise, what changes do I choose to make for next week?

Team

Balance between tasks at work can save time and energy. How many times do you sit in meetings and think, *I could be so much more productive with fewer meetings*? Suggest to your teams that they try to have fewer meetings and, when they do have meetings, that agendas are set and there are specific items to review. I find group brainstorming to be challenging, so I encourage our teams to send out the questions prior to the meeting and have one person collect responses so there is a detailed list to review in the meeting. For example, when we were developing a name for a product, we sent out communication to solicit ideas and then when the decision makers met we had a list of possible names to review. This approach saved time and energy.

Culture Infusion

Ensure your team knows you care about their work/life balance. Train supervisors to ask their team members how they can help facilitate better balance; what works for each of us is personal. Consider surveying employees on their work/life balance desires and implementing programs that will work for your business.

PRINCIPLE 4

Practice Effective Communication

The ability to communicate in the language, images, and emotions that evoke understanding, inspiration, and direction in the governed is the hallmark of effective leadership.

—Neil Fiore, *The Now Habit*

One of the most vital aspects of success in our personal and professional relationships is communication, the thread that connects us to each other. Without effective communication, ideas don't get shared or transferred, collaborations suffer, relationships break, and leaders become dictators.

When we hear the term "communication" we often think first of talking and of getting our point across, but this chapter will focus on the opposite angle: listening. When was the last time you truly listened to what the other person was saying? When someone is talking, are you thinking about your response? How many times do you get off subject because each person is interjecting to relate to the other?

We are often so focused on talking that we forget to listen to others first. We miss out when we don't listen, because taking time to listen actually sparks creativity and boosts esteem. Imagine interacting with peers who are motivated and inspired to do great work each day, and who enjoy each other! Listening is a big part of that.

Whether at work or at home with our significant other or our kids, listening is necessary for building trust. With trust come enhanced relationships that build a stable culture for continued success not only in the workplace but also in our personal lives. The way we are engaging in all aspects of life transfers into our workplaces.

As Henry Ford once remarked, "If there is any one secret of success, it lies in the ability to get the other person's point of view and see things from his angle as well as your own." Many times, it's not about being right; it's about taking the time to allow both parties to actually be heard.

In this chapter, we will look at what makes personal and workplace communication effective, and why it is such an important skill for personal and organizational well-being.

Part 1: Personal Communication

Personal communication is about how you as an individual engage with one or more others in an exchange of information. This information could include facts, emotions, signals, intentions, and a variety of other "messages" that are intended or not intended. Because of the complexity of communication, it is important to pay close attention to your own communication tendencies and to practice the art and science of listening (receiving) as well as offering information.

Active Listening

Effective personal communication requires *active* listening: making a conscious effort to hear not only the words that another person is saying but, more importantly, trying to understand the complete message being sent. Active listening is about engaging in the conversation in ways beyond just talking. In this section, we'll explore the following Tips for Active Listening:

1. Practice empathy

2. Focus attention

3. Show listening

4. Suspend judgment

5. Be responsive

As you will see with these tips, active listening does require effort, but it is also something you can learn through practice in a few key areas.

Practice Empathy

Empathy is where active listening starts. It's the ability to put yourself in someone else's shoes and see things from their perspective rather than yours. We often don't know what another person might be going through. For example, someone on our team who is typically on point may not be focused on a big deliverable today. We might react with anger, telling them how disappointed we are in their work, and that they better shape up for the next deliverable or they will be in trouble. How helpful do you think that is? Right—not very!

Instead, we could use an empathetic response and ask them how they are doing today, and if everything is okay since their work is not as great as usual. Maybe they had a fight with a loved one, found out someone close to them passed away, or had a leak in their home this morning that caused major damage. When you know this information, you can better understand their true situation and have a useful, direct conversation. They will also see that you care.

Empathy is challenging because we are also facing our own daily struggles and conflict. Yet if we could slow down and take a moment to empathize instead of judging in our relationships, they would go more smoothly. This takes patience and practice. Carl Rogers, a 20th-century humanist psychologist and the founder of person-centered psychotherapy, eloquently discussed in his theories, "Empathy is a special way of coming to know another and ourselves, a kind of attuning and understanding. When empathy is extended, it satisfies our needs and wish for intimacy, it rescues us from our feelings of aloneness."

Focus Attention

In this age of constant distraction, focusing your attention is a gift for both you and the person you're listening to. It does, however, require some discipline on your part.

You must not allow yourself to become distracted by whatever else may be going on around you. Checking email or texts, for example, during a conversation is a sure way to make the speaker feel you are not listening. Put away the phone and be attentive.

Resist the urge to think up counterarguments that you'll make when the other person stops speaking. Your only "job" when someone is speaking is to listen fully.

If you are bored, you will likely stop hearing what the other person is saying. Get curious instead, looking to find out from the speaker something you didn't know before (about them or the topic).

Pretend nothing else matters except the present moment and understanding the speaker—because that actually *is* all that matters right then.

Show Listening

Active listening is a two-way street. Let the speaker know without a doubt that you are fully listening. Have you ever told someone something very important to you, only to get radio silence and no expression from the listener? Even if the other person is really listening to you, if they don't show that to you, it can feel pretty terrible. Again, active listening needs to be *active*.

Give the speaker your focused attention and acknowledge their message both verbally and nonverbally. Respond with subtle encouragement by responding with "yes" or "I understand" or even just "mmm-hmm." Use body language such as smiling, nodding, a concerned or interested expression, or any other response to suggest without words, "Yes, I'm listening. I hear you. Go on."

Make sure that your responses are subtle enough to show that you are listening without bringing the focus of the conversation to yourself. Your goal is to help the speaker feel comfortable in sharing their ideas. Your chance to respond and be listened to will come soon!

Suspend Judgment

What usually happens when someone offers information or a suggestion? We try to decide if we agree with it or not. And if we disagree, we are quick to let that be known! However, the speaker may not want to continue if there is a feeling you are not in agreement before they have even finished communicating.

When we instead suspend judgment, we aren't concerned with agreeing or disagreeing; we just want to understand the other person's message. We allow the speaker to portray their message without interrupting them, being careful not to derail what they are saying.

My personal motto for communication is "Listen to understand." Believe me, I haven't always used this approach. I used to get in arguments all the time, convinced that I was being totally reasonable. However, as I look back, I see I was not. I was often in a blame game, judging and feeling that I was right and the other person was wrong. I now understand more clearly that we all play a role in each situation and we have to take accountability for that role even if it's not intentional. In the past, I wasn't listening, so I wasn't understanding the complete situation. Without the broader viewpoint of understanding, my conversations often turned into arguments and ongoing conflict.

Culture Infusion

I realized the importance of this change when I read don Miguel Ruiz's book *The Four Agreements*. The first of the four agreements is "Be Impeccable with Your Word. Speak with integrity. Say only what you mean. Avoid using the Word to speak against yourself or to gossip about others. Use the power of your Word in the direction of truth and love."[27]

This made me aware of how I was using the language of judgment, and it helped me switch my mindset away from judgment. I do strive to listen to understand, but I am far from perfect and sometimes I'm more successful than others!

Even if you do not agree with someone, be mindful and assert your opinions gracefully and in due time. Treat the other person with the respect and compassion you would also want. One practice that helps us suspend judgment is to resist making assumptions. When we make assumptions about a person or situation, we are basically saying that we already know what is really going on and don't need to verify our understanding with anyone else. We have already made our own judgment without all the facts and perspectives.

Making assumptions is basically making up stories without checking the facts. We might assume that our boss is ignoring us when s/he thought we prefer to work as independently as possible. We might assume that people are intentionally trying to hurt us when they had no idea we were upset. We might assume things about what others need or want. You can imagine how this can lead to poor communication.

In *The Four Agreements*, Agreement #3 offers powerful guidance on this topic: "Don't Make Assumptions. Find the courage to ask questions and to express what you really want. Communicate with others as clearly as you can to avoid misunderstandings, sadness and drama. With just this one agreement, you can completely transform your life."[28]

Which leads us to our next tip for active listening: be responsive.

Be Responsive

I talked earlier about giving subtle responses to show you're listening. This tip is about direct spoken responses that help clarify whether you have understood the speaker. Asking questions, paraphrasing, and summarizing what you heard back to the speaker will make a huge difference in shared understanding.

Ask Questions

The questioning process enables us to become more interested in what the other person is saying. Also, when we listen to someone respond to our question, we may see the situation more clearly, or—better yet—the person we are communicating with might come to their own resolution. Effective questions encourage others to continue forward.

Keep in mind that there is an art to asking questions. Questions can either open up or shut down a conversation. Which approach do you think is more effective: having a "learner" mindset or a "judger" mindset? (Hint: Reread the earlier "Suspend Judgment" section.)

The learner mindset focuses on questions that are proactive and foster new possibilities:

- What can we do about this?

- What is one thing that seems impossible? What would make it possible?

- How can we stay on track?

- What can we learn from this?

In the book *Just Listen* by Mark Goulston, he explains that these types of questions "move a person from a defensive, closed position or a selfish, excuse-making stance into an open, thinking attitude."[29]

On the other hand, judging questions are reactive and focus on the past. Be careful *not* to ask:

- Why did you fail again?

- Whose fault is this?

- Why can't you get this right?

- When will you learn? (Yes, rhetorical questions also have impact.)

Questions are powerful tools that can either hinder or catapult forward movement. As Albert Einstein said, "It is not that I'm so smart. But I stay with the questions much longer." He was constantly asking learner questions.

Take a moment to ask those *why, what,* and *what if* questions. Below is a list of potential learner questions to ask, either with your employees or modified for personal interactions:

- Why do you feel this happened?

- Could we go another direction?

- Are there untapped resources we could utilize?

- What happens if we shift our focus to...?

What are some other questions you could ask to encourage forward movement?

Verify Understanding

Another way to be directly responsive is to summarize or paraphrase back to the speaker what you heard, asking them to verify or correct what you understood. This might seem like an unnecessary step if you have followed all the active listening tips, but direct verification can still uncover unexpected misunderstandings.

Far too often, conflict arises when we don't understand the full picture. We are quick to make assumptions so we can move on to making decisions. If you have a conversation where information is exchanged, wrap it up with a summary statement. Summarizing will not only ensure accurate follow-through, it will help to ensure both parties are on the same page with shared understanding.

This shared understanding is important in any conversation, actually. Paraphrase back to the speaker what you heard to verify it is the message they intended to get across. In any conversation, you can verify understanding with statements such as:

- What I am hearing is...

- Sounds like you are saying...

- When you say..., do you mean...?

- So what we have agreed on is [fill in the blank]. Is that correct?

Yes, this careful attention and response does take some extra time, but I assure you it is well worth it! Shared understanding and clear communication save plenty of time and energy down the road by avoiding miscommunication, frustration, and conflict.

Open-Door Policy

As a leader, you can send an important communication message by having an open-door policy. We've all heard managers state that they have an open-door policy, but do they really mean it? Do *you* really mean it when you say it?

In your organization, make certain your employees know they can come and talk to anyone at any time—whether at the peer level, manager level, or executive level. By encouraging employees to communicate openly, issues will be identified and resolved, rather than building a culture that allows issues to fester.

As a leader, you are responsible for setting a good example by practicing active listening when anyone needs to discuss an issue or offer feedback to you. This means you turn away from your computer, focus your attention on the speaker, and truly seek to understand, using all five Tips for Active Listening. Of course, you can decide whether you can give the person your full attention right away or if you need to acknowledge them briefly and set a different time to have an in-depth conversation. The most important part is that they feel immediately acknowledged and valued.

REAL-LIFE EXAMPLE FROM AN ACTUALIZE SENIOR MANAGER

"When an employee (we'll call her Alice) approached me with a grievance she had about being over-committed within her practice group, I knew it was best to stop what I was doing and give her my full attention. As a senior manager in Human Resources since 2006, I realize the importance of being responsive to our employees' concerns and handling them with sensitivity and respect.

After listening carefully to her concerns, asking her clarifying questions, and repeating back to her what I was hearing about her concern, it was clear that Alice was feeling overwhelmed. She was working many hours and spinning in circles trying to get her job done while also dealing with many other factors in her personal life.

I decided to start with what things Alice could do to make more time available for herself, so that she would know that I understood that something needed to be done, and that she could confide in me at any time, knowing I would support her in finding a resolution to her issues.

I decided to reset her expectations by letting her know I have felt this way before as well, then shared what I did to handle the feeling of being overwhelmed by my day-to-day responsibilities. I told her how taking a break or two each day helped me to readjust priorities throughout the day, and that in doing so, I was able to focus and become more productive. As our firm culture encourages, taking a walk outside for fifteen minutes or taking five minutes to practice a breathing routine can help the mind to regroup and organize our daily activities.

After my conversation with Alice, we both committed to the accountability of doing these things for ourselves as a daily practice. Through this, I felt assured that Alice would continue to come to me to talk things out, or for guidance at any time, therefore endorsing our open-door policy at the firm."

The Four Gates Exercise

After you have done the important work of listening to understand, then what? You get to share your reactions with the speaker. When you offer your viewpoint, you can decide how to react by using an old Sufi tradition that advises us to speak only after our words have managed to pass through four gates, as follows:

1. At the first gate, we ask ourselves, "Are these words *true?*" If so, we let them pass on; if not, back they go.

2. At the second gate, we ask, "Are they *necessary?*" If so, we let them pass on; if not, back they go.

3. At the third gate, we ask, "Are they *beneficial?*" If so, we let them pass on; if not, back they go.

4. At the fourth gate, we ask, "Are they *kind?*" If so, we let them pass on; if not, back they go.

If the answer to any of these is no, then what you are about to say should be left unsaid. If the answer to all of these questions is yes, then the words you are about to say are most likely respectful and important. Speak them.

Part 2: Corporate Communications

Up to this point, I've talked mostly about 1–1 personal communication. Equally important, however, is the communication between your organization and its employees. This communication has a huge impact on your company's organizational culture. Does your organization actively listen to employees? It needs to. In this section, I provide several ways to enhance your *organizational* communication through active listening.

The way your organization communicates to employees has a significant impact on the health of your organization. Let's say you add or adjust a policy, or make other changes, big or small, around the organization. If you communicate the change properly, employees will have an easier time adjusting to the change—whether or not they agree with it.

On the other hand, poor communication regarding new policies or changes can be detrimental to overall morale and take away from productivity as employees struggle to adjust. The water-cooler talk goes rampant: "Can you believe that they took all our vending and soda machines away?" "Have you noticed the food portions in the cafeteria are smaller but cost more?" "Did you hear that they are going to let 20 percent of the workforce go and my group is the first one targeted?" These conversations go on and on, building stress and gaining momentum each day.

Communication around why changes are being made can give your employees relief. When we know why something is happening, it is much easier to digest.

Examples of Effective Internal Communications

Let's go back to those water-cooler concerns from before. Think about how those conversations would change if the following communications had been sent out before the changes occurred:

> In an effort to cultivate a culture of wellness, we are removing the soda and vending machines and replacing them with healthier options. We know it might take some time to get used to. We care about our employees and want you to have the best possible choices to fuel your body.

> We have offered a subsidized cafeteria for as long as we have been in business and we know you enjoy the perk (we all do!). Yet, we are looking at all expenses in an effort to improve our bottom line. We recognize now that we cannot sustain all the choices we previously made and apologize for any inconvenience, knowing that change is difficult, especially if we stop offering something you really enjoyed. We have made the following changes...

We want to address the rumors around the latest workforce reductions and the groups that will be impacted. We will provide specifics by next week. Again, please bear with us as we are doing the best we can to sustain the firm with the most productivity possible. As you have seen, we have been losing money in this part of the organization and do not see a change in the market to support this group in the foreseeable future. We know you may be concerned with your job security and we will be working to transfer some of you to other parts of the organization. For those that we unfortunately must let go, we are offering severance packages and any assistance we can with providing a positive reference for your next employment opportunities.

While these communications don't take away the difficult news, they do show employees that you care enough to be honest with them.

How to Use Various Communications Methods Effectively

Frequent and meaningful communication will foster fresh ideas, keep everyone on the same page, and give your employees the information they need to make decisions. Use a variety of communications methods to keep information both interesting and consistent.

Some examples include:

- **Newsletters:** Include relevant company information, employee highlights (list birthdays for the month, highlight an employee and share their biography or an interesting fact), information on industry training and conferences, team appreciation and success sharing, and wellness tips.

- **All-hands meetings or conference calls:** Hold these meetings at least monthly, and rotate ownership of the meetings with management and staff to encourage participation and fresh ideas.

- **Blast emails:** Send these out to all employees for real-time updates on the company. Celebrate wins and successes.

- **Check-in meetings:** Schedule at least monthly calls or meetings with your team both individually and as a group. Having times to communicate is integral to everyone being heard. One client has a "10x10" strategy for her direct report meetings: she will speak for ten minutes and her direct report will speak for ten minutes, ensuring each side is heard. She says it has been extremely effective over the years and she has had high tenure with direct reports because they always have a forum in which to speak up.

- **A "get to know you" budget:** Encourage sharing of information across staff and with the management team by giving each team a budget to get to know someone better through lunch meetings, coffee breaks, etc.

- **Show gratitude:** Suggest a week of random acts of kindness exchanges with team members and external customers (nothing monetary allowed).

Conclusion

By focusing on compassionate and continuous communication, we can better know our employees, quickly come to resolutions, and build a firm that nourishes our employees all year long. Effective communication skills—whether in soliciting information, dealing with a challenge, or announcing an organizational change—foster success in life, work, and relationships.

> "In this holographic world, everyone is you and you are always talking to yourself."
>
> **—Debbie Ford**

In any interaction, you can improve communication by using the following Tips for Active Listening:

1. Practice empathy

2. Focus attention

3. Show listening

4. Suspend judgment

5. Be responsive

MIND-EXPANDING EXPERIENCES

Personal

1. When was the last time you had difficulty communicating either personally or in a business situation? Write down your side of the situation. Let it all out; hold nothing back. Describe the situation and what was difficult about it.

2. Next, switch sides and write from the other person's perspective.

3. Then, ask yourself the following questions and write out the answers:

    - What was my role in the conflict?

    - What is it that I am unwilling to be responsible for in this situation? What would happen if I took responsibility?

    - Where could I have been more empathetic?

BONUS:

Tell the person you wrote about above that you are sorry for your role in the conflict. Practice being 100 percent responsible for everything that transpires; pause to notice your role in challenging communications.

Team

Use this exercise to enhance listening and empathy skills.

1. Split up into groups of two.

2. Choose a topic for the pairs to talk about. It can be related to a specific business topic or personal exploration. For example, "What is one issue you are currently facing and how would you like to positively resolve it?"

3. Have one person talk for 2–3 minutes while the other listens fully, staying engaged without talking.

4. Next, have the talker and listener switch roles for another 2–3 minutes.

5. Finish with giving the pairs 2–3 minutes to discuss with each other any thoughts that came up during their time of listening.

Culture Infusion

Take an inventory of your organization's style of communication. How can you enhance and infuse into your organization the suggestions in this chapter? How can you lead by example in using effective communication strategies in all your interactions? A few options are to facilitate or hire an outside firm to lead communication experiences.

At Actualize, I facilitate theme weeks in which I will send tidbits of information each day for a week or a month to spark ideas for better communication. We also have used improv-facilitated sessions to encourage listening in a different way. The first rule in improv is to say, "Yes, and." As we are communicating, we can go back to those principles and be playful with others. For example, instead of stewing because someone did not listen to my idea I can playfully say, "What you meant to say was, 'Yes, and I hear your idea, let's discuss'." I will typically get a chuckle as they remember they are not supposed to initially say no to others' ideas.

PRINCIPLE 5

Handle Conflict Directly, Openly, and Immediately

A problem is a chance to do your best.

—Duke Ellington

If we encountered every interaction filled with peace, love, and harmony, what a beautiful world we would live in. The reality is that no matter how smoothly life is going, we will still face conflict during our journey. The opportunity for growth is in how we navigate those twists in the road. As Maya Angelou frequently said in her work, "If you don't like something, change it. If you can't change it, change your attitude." No matter who started a conflict, you have the power to change the outcome, beginning with how you communicate in a tense situation.

When there are issues in your team, remember that every problem is an opportunity to make positive change. Nobody wants to mess up, yet it happens; we are all normal and all make mistakes.

Take the approach that everything is a learning opportunity and work with your employees on how to improve rather than running them into the ground and making them feel even worse. If they know you care and support them even in hard times, you will have their loyalty. Most times, something is personally going on with an individual or they simply don't have the skills needed.

This principle challenges us to view difficult interactions as a life puzzle with useful lessons at each turn. We will explore how to use effective communication to pause to pivot to positive possibilities. I will focus here on workplace situations, but this section applies to personal situations as well.

In Principle 4: Practice Effective Communication, we discussed communication strategies, and in this principle we use those same strategies to deal with conflict. In order to understand the needs and desires of our employees, we need to

> **"Whenever you are pointing your finger at someone, notice that there are always three fingers pointing back at you."**
>
> **—Anonymous**

provide a healthy, welcoming culture in which employees feel safe enough to be honest. I will talk in more detail in Principle 7: Regularly Conduct Employee Surveys about using surveys as a more formal way to gather feedback; in this principle, we'll focus on everyday interactions. Knowing how to offer space and to communicate effectively without offending others is an essential competency for all members of a firm, at all levels, starting with management. The most effective organizations lead by example. When delicate situations are brought to management, how they are handled sends a strong message to others, either encouraging or discouraging them from expressing themselves openly. We all want to be thoroughly heard with compassion, and leaders must show us how it's done.

How can an organization be successful in creating a culture in which employees feel safe to speak truthfully? The first step is to instill accountability in all scenarios. As the Managing Director of Human Resources and Operations, I consistently reiterate, "I want to understand what is going on, yet remember we all play a role in the situation. What is your role; how are you accountable?" I then remind the individual that we do not tolerate blaming in our firm because we all play a part in each situation. This may sound harsh, yet it has worked for the positive time and time again over the years.

The second step is to meet conflict head on, face-to-face when possible. If you are part of the conflict situation, suggest that everyone involved meet in person or via conference call. In today's highly informational and technological environment, spoken communication is more important than ever. Pick up the phone or meet in person when possible, and enjoy more rewarding relationships and bonds.

In a recent scenario at Actualize, we had a team divided in discord. We needed to reestablish open, trusting communication, so we used a technique inspired by Thich Nhat Hanh's Watering Flowers exercise (from his books *A Pebble in Your Pocket* and *The Art of Communicating*) and consisting of three simple prompts:

Culture Infusion

1. **What are you grateful for?**

   Actualize Situation: By starting the meeting with gratitude, the vibe immediately shifted from negative to positive. Each person shared gratitude after gratitude, which contagiously spread, opening the space for interpersonal connection as the team erupted into laughter.

2. **What do you regret?**

   Actualize Situation: As we moved to regret, the mood sobered, yet each person who had a regret was still able to sincerely apologize to those impacted. Forgiveness came quickly, showing that a simple apology goes a long way. For instance, one team member expressed regret for not checking his work, which had caused another team member to stay up all night correcting the error. Before this, the "all-nighter" team member had not known whether anyone really appreciated his sacrificing a night's sleep. He was content with simply being seen, and readily accepted the apology.

3. **How were your feelings hurt?**

   Actualize Situation: By the time we reached this question, all team members were feeling compassion for their co-workers and many complaints that had been voiced before did not surface. The genuine conversations around regrets had satisfied the majority of the hurt feelings. Team members expressed the few remaining hurt feelings with intentional consideration and in pure honesty.

In most cases, taking the time to ensure all parties are heard is enough to move forward in a positive light. Below are some additional suggestions on managing and resolving conflict at any level in the organization:

- Shut down gossip. If someone starts speaking about a co-worker, do not participate; divert the conversation to a positive.

- Seek resolution by guiding understanding, agreement, and consensus.

- Listen fully. Often the person with the complaint will resolve their own issue if given the opportunity to vent privately to a kind ear. I know we discussed this previously, yet in my experience fully listening is challenging and therefore worth mentioning again.

There are no guarantees that your communication efforts will be met with total compliance and agreement. However, as long as you genuinely strive to understand each other, and are cordial and respectful, you can still have a successful exchange.

The 3P Method: Pause to Pivot to Positive

At Actualize, we use what we call the 3P Method as a guideline for handling conflict, and we encourage our team to think through these steps when negative emotions arise. We all strive to Pause to Pivot to the Positive, using those three steps to bring together our individual awareness, open and honest communication (with active listening), and shared resolution of the issue by moving forward together.

Step 1: Pause to Conquer Negativity

How many times a day do you catch yourself immediately thinking a negative thought? How many times do you say to others, "Don't be so defensive"? As humans, our natural tendency is a bias towards negativity caused by parts of our brains that are quickly triggered to "avoid harm" while slower to react to "pursuing rewards." The Genetic Science Learning Center in Utah explains how cells communicate during fight or flight: "When our senses perceive an environmental stress such as danger or a threat, cells in the nervous and endocrine systems work closely together to prepare the body for action. Often referred to as the fight or flight or stress response, this remarkable example of cell communication elicits instantaneous and simultaneous responses throughout the body."[30] Negativity is part of our composition. How, then, do we shift our focus?

We will explore an example of how my team traversed our negative emotions and learned how to take the higher, more positive road. One of my internal team's key responsibilities is to recruit and hire talent. Being in a niche market, we take pride in our abilities to equip our client-facing team with the best resources. Therefore, when we heard the client-facing team say on a resource call, "I have no confidence that your team can provide us with the resources we need," our fight response came to the surface. But what if the following had been said instead? "I want to help your team devise a solution to ensure we have the resources we need."

Which one feels better? Notice how you immediately feel different simply with a change in verbal messaging. Have you ever realized you respond more rapidly to problems than possibilities? (Remember the "fight or flight"?) When we are stuck on the negative, we fail to notice the positives, and a tornado of feelings may spiral out of control. In our team example, the first statement immediately put us on the defense because we weren't aware that we apparently hadn't delivered on our goal of team satisfaction. Both sides dove right into a nasty battle of blame, which did not feel good and was not best for our firm. We reacted when we should have paused.

Allowing the negative feelings without reacting is certainly not easy. It takes time to remember that negative tendencies are natural, and it takes practice to realize that bottling up those feelings is not healthy. When the blood is boiling, make an effort not to react. Instead, both parties should *pause* to settle their feelings and allow the tension to pass.

Step 2: Pivot Out of the Negative Spiral

When we are consumed with our reactive feelings, moving to the positive can be a steep mountain to climb, whether in a group setting or simply working through our own anger or frustration. Going back to my team and the initial negative comment— "I have no confidence that your team can provide us with the resources we need"—we can *pivot* out of the negative spiral by exploring what happened. What is our side? What would an outsider's perspective be? Can we identify why there was a challenge? For example, have each team member ponder each perspective individually and then discuss as a group:

- **Our Side:** We were not clear on the exact resources the client-facing team needed, nor the timing or the urgency, because we were getting direction from multiple sources.

- **Outsider's Perspective:** The client-facing team was working overtime and submitted a job requirement; they thought they had done what was needed.

- **Why a Challenge:** Both sides thought they were doing the right thing, but without fully communicating with each other. When there was finally a discussion, both sides were already frustrated, hence all the negative emotions.

In this scenario, do you think either side really wanted to fight or to fail the other? That possibility might sound ridiculous, but since that negative tendency is part of our composition, it is extremely important to acknowledge it and practice pausing before we react. Once my team got over the initial fight response, and remembered we are all on the same larger team, we were all able to have the difficult—and clarifying—conversation that came about by walking through the above exercise. Both sides left feeling relief at being heard and had a repaired compassion towards each other. If you are working solo, ask yourself, "What positive outcome could occur with a pivot?"

Step 3: Consider Positive Possibilities

During the situation with my team, after pivoting out of the negative, we wrapped up the exercise as a team with identifying the opportunities to move forward in finding the appropriate people to fill our resource needs. Since then, we have been having more regular calls to ensure both sides are briefed on the daily changes in project needs. Henry David Thoreau wrote in his *Journal*, "We are always paid for our suspicion by finding what we suspect."[31] If we expect to see the negative, we will see it; if we instead look for the positive, then that's what we will see. In the case of shifting to the positive in a personal situation, list out all the positive possible alternatives to move forward.

By changing our focus, we can discover the silver lining in any scenario. In our situation at Actualize, the positives now shine bright as we are expanding into exciting new areas of growth together. Playing the blame game is never productive. The recipe of success is instead held together with teamwork and accountability.

Conclusion

Life would be boring without contrasting personalities, views, and opinions. My brother Chad and I are a prime example of that. I tend to see the bright side, and he tends to focus on how it can be done better; both are necessary views. We have found that when we use the 3P Method as a guiding communication technique, there are fewer conflicts with our communication and in our team.

The next time you are faced with a challenge, use the 3P Method and Pause to Pivot to Positive:

- Step 1: **Pause** to conquer negativity

- Step 2: **Pivot** out of the negative spiral

- Step 3: Consider **positive** possibilities

This will help quickly shift your energy towards helpful actions based on teamwork and agreement.

MIND-EXPANDING EXPERIENCES

Personal

Document the 3P Method with a recent scenario you experienced. Use the following questions to guide you:

1. What negative feeling did you experience? Why?

2. How could you have changed your negative response?

3. What positive could or did happen from this situation?

Team

Practice the Watering Flowers exercise with the following questions:

1. What are you grateful for?

2. What do you regret?

3. How were your feelings hurt?

Start with a small group in which you would like to strengthen relationships. There does not necessarily have to be conflict. Many times, I use this exercise at the dinner table with my kids to enhance our communication and ensure we are resolving any conflicts. As you gain confidence with the exercise, use it in your business interactions as well as personal relationships. We all want to feel heard and appreciated.

Culture Infusion

Implement the 3P Method in your firm. The concept is easy and we have found that having a common way of dealing with conflict levels the playing field and many times fends off conflict before it starts.

PRINCIPLE 6

Focus on Your People

True love exists in business. It's when employee and employer are amazingly grateful to have each other. We should all have love at work.

—Simon Sinek

The Actualize company tagline is "Our expertise and commitment driving your success." This tagline, with its focus on our clients, is only possible because of our motto, "Our people first." Initially, we used the tagline as a reminder to keep our focus on the success of our clients, but in time the meaning of that tagline has changed. We are definitely still dedicated and committed to our clients' success, but that now starts with dedication and commitment to our team first.

When Actualize was faced with low morale and uncertainty after a partner left the firm, we shifted our focus first and foremost from our clients to our *people*. Although this shift may seem counterintuitive, now that our company is full of happier employees, we naturally provide an even greater customer experience, time and time again.

The three key factors in this principle are hiring the right people, providing a robust and generous benefits package, and prioritizing wellness. Having happy and healthy employees allows them to shine for our clients. In this chapter, I will share some of the programs I have implemented at Actualize that have helped us focus on our people and embed this principle into our organizational culture. As you read about these programs, I suggest you ponder how you may be able to shift your focus to your people and potentially use some of these suggestions in your own organization.

Hiring the Right Team

With our tenure the highest ever, and our attrition decreasing year to year, we are often asked what our secret is. First, we do not hire someone at Actualize unless we are 100 percent confident in our decision.

We begin by conducting an intensive interviewing and reference-checking process. Our lead recruiter has been with the firm since 2006 and understands our needs in terms of skill set and also knows what it takes to be a successful consultant. We have a series of interviews candidates must pass through including screening, behavioral, and technical. If the candidate and our lead recruiter feel they are a match for Actualize after these interviews, I then interview the candidate to ensure they are ready to interview with one of the partners. When I interview, I focus on whether they will be a good fit for our team and I discuss our benefits and culture. This is my favorite conversation I have at work because I love bragging on all our positive qualities. I am confident that if a recruit has gotten this far, I can sell them on working with our team.

The partners in the firm joke about "the Kerry gut"—my intuition about new talent. Over the years, I have honed my skills on picking up on the smallest details. For example, if a recruit does not treat my team or me with the utmost respect, that is a sign they will not treat our clients with respect. We believe you should treat everyone with the same level of courtesy, no matter their level within the firm.

Taking the time to find the exact match is well worth the time and energy. If you have any doubt, the answer is no. Others agree with our approach. In his book *Anything You Want*, Derek Sivers makes an easy-to-remember point: "If it isn't a clear yes, then it's a clear no."[32] It took time for us to become more patient and more selective and pay attention to all the subtle details of our conversations with potential new hires. Now, if one team member identifies a red flag, the next will dig deeper. We truly act as a team in our hiring decisions. As we discussed before, this is another area where sharing effective communication is important, so all team members are aware of each other's assessment of the candidate. As Jim Collins says in his book *Good to Great*, "the right person is based more upon character traits and innate capabilities than specific knowledge, background, or skills."[33]

Providing a Robust and Generous Benefits Package

You know that your company's success depends on its people, and your benefits package needs to reflect that. Provide best-in-class benefits to show that you understand the importance of your employees at all levels. With a little creativity, you can expand your benefits package to provide more than is expected, allowing you to really walk your talk in regards to your corporate culture of wellness and your focus on people.

Actualize has a robust package for retirement, health insurance, and paid time off. In addition, I have helped Actualize add important perks that are above and beyond the usual, including different wellness benefits, educational opportunities, time off, and various rewards. Not only do the employees appreciate the extra special treatment, but they are also enhancing skills that directly improve our company results. As I share some of our unique benefits in this chapter, consider the why, how, and what of benefits you might offer your employees.

Rewards

As with many other things in a healthy and vibrant company culture, rewards can be a two-way street. Your employees are your greatest resource, so determine ways they can help grow the business and increase the bottom line. People do want to help their company be successful, and they will appreciate the chance to step up, especially when rewarded appropriately.

Some ideas for additional ways employees can provide value include:

- Write articles to promote the firm's expertise

- Provide marketing assistance

- Interview new members of the team

- Provide strong referrals (who become new hires)

- Bring in additional clients or make additional sales

- Take initiative on successful above-and-beyond projects and roles related to their job

- Create a new product or innovative idea

Then, make sure to reward employees for going above and beyond. Credit them with a byline for articles they write, provide referral bonuses and sales incentives, thank them publicly with a company email blast and a gift certificate or extra time off for stellar marketing and onboarding help, and provide performance bonuses. You might even consider asking an employee what would feel like a right-sized reward for their extra work, and negotiate from there. Bottom line: make sure employees know that you appreciate everything extra they do.

Training and Education Benefits

Training and education is one of the most important benefits you can offer. Giving employees a chance to enhance their current skills and learn new ones helps them stay interested and engaged, and your company benefits from greater retention and even more capable employees. With a healthy dose of challenge, our brains work better and we feel sharper and more confident. A culture of learning also encourages employees to have an interest in learning from others, leading to better collaboration and teamwork. Instead of competing against each other's knowledge, they are more likely to respect and seek out each other's expertise.

Actually, learning is a skill itself. Think of how often things change in an industry or organization. When employees are skilled at learning, the organization is too. Companies whose employees continue to learn are much more sustainable because they adapt quickly rather than being left behind. This need to prepare for near-constant change also fuels creativity and innovation in an organization, which leads to more learning, and the positive cycle continues.

Training and Education: What's the Difference?

A comprehensive learning benefit includes both training and education benefits. Training is about *doing* something, and education is about *knowing* something. While training and education usually overlap at least a little, the focus of each is different. To learn new computer skills, for example, we would attend a training that included hands-on practice. To learn about the mortgage industry, however, we would take a class to learn information rather than a hands-on skill.

Following are examples of both training and education benefits you might offer your employees:

Training Benefits:

Encourage your employees to attend trainings, industry seminars, or conferences of interest, both in-house and off-site, and offer reimbursement.

- Develop a list of trainings your employees might be interested in based on the skills you are trying to build within your firm. By doing this research for your employees, they can then simply scan the list and choose one.

- Offer your employees an annual training budget and encourage them to use the entire budget each year.

Culture Infusion

- Implement a leadership training program. Either hire outside firms or conduct training internally to ensure everyone is working together and learning lessons from each situation.

- Solicit ideas from employees on other trainings they want you to offer. They might even end up providing you with the company training schedule for the year.

- Consider encouraging employees to use some of their training allotment to gain personal skills. This will keep them satisfied and energized for company work, and shows you are interested in their holistic well-being. For example, I use some of my own training budget for yoga teacher training and wellness retreats.

Education Benefits:

Encourage your employees to also attend educational seminars, workshops, and classes, both in-house and off-site, and offer reimbursement.

- Hold trainings to teach your employees about the history and culture of your firm and how they can be successful there. Ensure they are educated on how to portray the company to others, including the firm's elevator speech, and what is necessary for them to continue to grow within the firm.

- Hold regular brown-bag lunches (or "lunch and learn" sessions) for employees to focus on specific topics. Ask employees to lead sessions about topics in their expertise.

Get creative with these, using a game format or team competitions.

- Encourage employees to take a class at a local college or attend learning sessions in the community. Again, encourage them to take both job-related and personal-interest classes.

Prioritize Wellness from the Inside Out

We all face daily changes in our industries, and we need to be able to react *wisely* to outside markets and external pressures. However, the most effective and lasting cultural changes are made from the inside out. Consider turning your corporate focus upside down by turning it inside out.

One of the first things we did at Actualize to increase our focus on our people was to enhance our wellness program. Although wellness is often an afterthought in a company, we chose to make it a priority by including wellness perks as a significant part of our benefits package. We want our employees to know that we don't only care about their work, but we also care about their health and happiness.

We were not willing, however, to just offer a quick fix or two. Knowing that a firm's culture needs a strong foundation, we set our sights on creating a culture of wellness from the inside out (including all levels of leadership). Changes in company culture take time and energy to cultivate, but we were willing to invest those resources. Turns out that investment was wise, as we have found that prioritizing wellness is a cultural shift that benefits the organization as a whole with happier, healthier, and more engaged employees.

For a wellness program to be successful, perks need to be chosen based on what employees actually want and need (discovered by conducting surveys, which we will cover in detail in Principle 7: Regularly Conduct Employee Surveys). Plenty of firms are focused on offering wellness benefits, yet they may be doing it simply to check the box, without establishing what will work for all their employees. For example, holding one wellness fair a year with free health screenings is a wellness offering, but it is just one day per year and may not include all employees if some cannot attend. At Actualize, we have wellness challenges and programs year-round to keep our team engaged in a healthy mindset. Our goal is to cultivate wellness year-round in a way that works for all employees.

> **A healthier person is a happier person, and a happier person is a more effective employee.**

To truly create a cultural shift, the core of the firm must support the cause with this inside-out approach. For example, Google has an entire training program on meditation, including a book titled *Search Inside Yourself* about meditation and how to incorporate it into the workplace. This book was written by Chade-Meng Tan, who used to be Google's "Jolly Good Fellow (which nobody can deny)"—a job title that started out as a joke, then became his actual title!

If a company as successful as Google believes in the importance of an inside-out approach, it makes sense to follow their lead. Let's look at some examples at Actualize.

Nourishment

It is important to provide ongoing support towards healthy eating choices. You can do this by making some simple changes in what your organization offers as nourishment. If it's there, it will be eaten, so the first step is to get rid of the temptations of unhealthy options such as vending machines stocked with soda, chips, cookies, and candy bars. Start fresh by offering more healthy options to choose from such as granola bars, nuts, and dried fruits. For catered meetings or events, present a variety of wholesome and satisfying food that will fuel employees for the remainder of the day. Instead of contributing to sugar highs and lows, you can help create balanced and healthy employees.

Tips for Healthier Meetings

Commit to providing healthy options for meetings of all sizes. Instead of donuts, cookies, and pizza, consider the following options:

- **Daytime meeting:** Provide a salad bar with a variety of greens and toppings. Locate a local restaurant to cater (such as Sweetgreen or Salad Creations), or order from the salad menu of a favorite lunch restaurant like Panera. Provide fruit as a sweet option after the meal and only offer water (no soda needed!).

- **Happy hour:** Select appetizers that are fresh and lean: skewers of meat and veggies, crudité platters, fresh fruit, seafood, hummus. As an alternative for those that do not drink alcohol, provide flavored seltzer water.

- **Off-site event:** Have the event catered with healthy options such as a veggie stir fry, carving station for lean meats, and fresh fruit and sorbet for dessert.

- **Walk-and-talk:** Encourage meeting while walking if there are only two people attending.

If you want to provide even more support, have experts come in and talk about nourishment or have a nutritionist available to speak to your employees as needed. You don't need to *be* an expert, you can simply *provide* one.

Wellness Benefits

Offer a variety of wellness perks and survey employees to determine what they are most interested in receiving. Below are some options:

- **Wellness dollars:** Employees are free to spend these at their leisure on anything related to overall well-being such as gym memberships, massage, personal training, classes, or equipment for their home gym.

- **On-site movement:** Offer classes during working hours to support physical movement throughout the day. Again, it is best to survey the workforce and offer classes in the most popular choices. In some firms yoga might be popular, while others may prefer a running or walking group or a weight-training class.

- **Group interaction:** Kick-start team inclusion by doing a wellness challenge such as focusing on nourishment or movement for a set time period. Offer prizes and the opportunity to come together as a group to discuss simple changes and realizations.

- **Health news and suggestions:** Distribute frequent communication on health and wellness using a variety of media and formats including articles, videos, quotes, facts, and cartoons.

- **Wellness fair:** Host at least one wellness fair each year and bring in vendors to offer a sample of healthy food and products. Have movement classes as part of the fair and give free chair massages. Provide raffles to give away wellness prizes such as massages, gym memberships, glass water bottles, etc. Another option for a wellness fair is to offer health screenings.

At Actualize, we infuse wellness into our culture. In fact, we have been nominated as one of the Healthiest Companies in the DC Metro Area. After attending the award ceremony, one of our managers stated, "One thing that stood out to me in hearing about different wellness programs is that where the protocol is to offer healthy programs, health is incorporated into the culture at Actualize. Healthy is not about the program that Actualize offers, health is embedded into who we are as a firm. And, [I] really appreciate the support and encouragement to be the healthiest I can be."

Bottom line, overall well-being drives success, whether personally or professionally. At the employer level, simply take the approach of going inside out and putting employees at the core of every decision. It will come back tenfold with loyalty and dedication because we tend to put energy into that which feels good.

The Company That Plays Together Stays Together

In addition to healthy nourishment options at Actualize, our wellness benefits include company-wide wellness challenges throughout the year. We have discovered that we are quite motivated by healthy competition! We like to keep our challenges fresh, so we change our themes. In one example, we used the program Daily Endorphins to track points earned in categories such as fitness, time for yourself, and healthy eating choices. Another time, we focused on movement and fun to reach a broader employee population.

Having seen how easily we get caught up in the stress of work and family demands, we decided to add fun as a wellness theme. While some professionals might consider fun a frivolous distraction from work, studies have shown quite the opposite. For example, in the *New York Times* article **"Scientists Hint at Why Laughter Feels So Good,"** James Gorman reported on a study of why laughter is so important to our health and well-being: "The answer, reports Robin Dunbar, an evolutionary psychologist at Oxford, is not the intellectual pleasure of cerebral humor, but the physical act of laughing. The simple muscular exertions involved in producing the familiar ha, ha, ha, he said, trigger an increase in endorphins, the brain chemicals known for their feel-good effect."[34]

In addition to incorporating fun into our wellness challenges, we advocate play upon meeting certain designated milestones, or through Lunch and Play, which I mentioned earlier, where we have a mini tournament of Jenga, checkers, or Connect Four. Get creative with how the winner can be recognized, such as bragging rights until the next tournament or giving them a pass for the week to skip out on a standing meeting or a task that is undesirable yet has to get done. We will discuss more on play in Principle 9: Encourage Team Connection.

Appreciation

As with laughter, our emotions have a direct impact on our physical health, so we emphasize appreciation as an important part of our firm's culture of wellness. We even have a section in our newsletter to give our team an opportunity to appreciate each other. We also spotlight employee and client successes.

Appreciation is a mindset that sets the tone for positive perspective in the present moment. In his book *How to Win Friends and Influence People*, Dale Carnegie notes that one of the fundamental techniques for handling people is to "give honest and sincere appreciation."[35] You might think your co-workers don't need to hear your appreciation, but psychologist and physician William James said, "The deepest craving of human nature is the need to be appreciated." To be successful, then, appreciation must span to our employer, boss, direct reports, and co-workers—our team. Appreciation, first and foremost, is integral to approaching each unique situation.

If you have conflict with a direct report, start with saying, "I really appreciate your efforts on this project, and I know you are giving it your best." Next, give the feedback to help with growth. "I would like to help you with this project; where could I add value? Have you thought about bringing other team members together for more collaboration?" Compare this to starting with, "I don't think this project is going well. You need to bring in other team members to help you." Always highlight the other person's value, and strive to support rather than tear down.

Charles Schwab said in his book *Guide to Financial Independence*, "I never criticize anyone. I believe in giving a person incentive to work. So, I am anxious to praise but loath to find fault. If I like anything, I am hearty in my approbation and lavish in my praise."[36] Appreciation can be helpful in a variety of situations. Imagine going to your boss with the intention to ask for a promotion. Instead of taking an entitled approach, start from a place of appreciation, explaining why you enjoy your job and how you feel you can add more value in the role you desire. Chances are that you will be listened to more fully with this tactic.

Appreciation has another important benefit to all parties involved: it simply makes you feel good. Positive, appreciative energy is a great boost for the organization, improving collaboration, communication, and overall performance.

A closely related topic is something called asset-based thinking (ABT), an approach depicted in the book *Lead Positive: What Highly Effective Leaders See, Say, and Do* by Kathryn D. Cramer. Asset-based thinking, Cramer explains, means "to look at yourself and the world through the eyes of what is working, what strengths are present, and what potentials are. Conversely, deficit-based thinking means to look at yourself and the world in terms of what is not working, what is lacking, and the gaps between where you are and where you want to be."[37]

Cramer uses former New York City Mayor Rudy Giuliani as an example of ABT leadership. In a press conference in the aftermath of 9/11, Giuliani stated, "I don't think we want to speculate on the number of casualties. The effort now has to be to save as many people as possible." As a result, there was an outpouring of volunteers at Ground Zero that saved an estimated twenty thousand civilian lives. Cramer described this event: "Note how Giuliani saw and focused on amazing acts of heroism amid the horrific aftermath of the attacks. More important, he communicated the importance and value of that heroism to the world. By biasing his attention toward the positive and possible, he led a successful rescue operation."[38]

You can choose to focus on the mistakes, the broken processes, and everything that isn't working well—and create a culture of disgruntled, fearful employees. But I suggest that as leaders we instead focus on the lessons to be learned, the possibility to improve operations, and the positive side of how to work together. Let's focus on the bright side of the challenge and what our employees are getting right. A team that feels empowered by their leadership will in turn take more pride and personal accountability in their work.

Conclusion

In order to serve and delight clients, employees need to be motivated and energized. Start from the inside out by focusing on your people and you will see happy, healthy employees as a result:

- Prioritize wellness in your benefits package
- Provide healthy food options at your offices, meetings, and events
- Gather your employees around fun wellness challenges
- Encourage appreciation and asset-based thinking
- Extend your kindnesses and considerations to possible recruits as well as employees

The result? I'll let this comment by an Actualize senior consultant speak for itself: "I want to express my gratitude and tell you how thankful I am for working with this great group of professionals that make up the Actualize family. By far the best company I've ever worked for. Thanks everybody for all your help and the positive attitude that you bring on a daily basis."

The key is to lead by example and provide an environment in which everyone can be successful. When everyone is on a healthy track, team morale is high.

MIND-EXPANDING EXPERIENCES

Personal

This exercise is focused on practicing appreciation. Any time you are feeling a negative emotion, pause for a moment and complete the following exercise.

1. Notice how you are feeling right now.

2. List five aspects you appreciate about your current job.

3. List five people you appreciate at your current job. For each person, list at least one thing you appreciate about them.

4. Notice again how you are feeling right now.

You probably feel at least a little bit better now than you did before starting this exercise, just because you thought about things and people you appreciate. There is always something to appreciate, even if it is simply that we are gainfully employed with a stable company or that we like our co-workers.

Team

Schedule a play date with your team: play games at lunch, go to a sporting event, take a painting class, or get out and move together on a walk-and-talk. Survey team members on what they want to do, and use their feedback to choose the event.

Culture Infusion

How can you focus more on your people? List at least three options. Which one can you implement first? What steps are required? When will you plan to roll it out?

PRINCIPLE 7

Regularly Conduct Employee Surveys

*The day soldiers stop bringing you their problems
is the day you have stopped leading them.*

—General Colin Powell

An important way to focus on your people is for your organization to actively listen to employees through anonymous surveys. Employees have direct experience with the inner and outer workings of the organization, so ask them what they think of how things are working (or not!). They know if the well-worn organizational paths are efficiencies or ruts, and they often have useful ideas of ways to make things even better. The internal operations team can review programs, processes, procedures, and systems on their own, but they will not be effective conducting these reviews in a vacuum; they *must* focus on open communication to gauge the pulse of employees.

Employees who are able to contribute ideas of their own to the firm will be happier with the results of changes or new initiatives. Your organization will also be able to more accurately provide the support and opportunities that employees actually want. To keep employees engaged and motivated, ask them for their experiences, opinions, and suggestions.

Some of you are probably rolling your eyes, thinking about all the surveys you have taken over the years with few—if any—changes actually made based on your feedback. You are right that surveys that only gather information are not useful. To make them effective, your organization must also provide detailed results back to your team and create an implementation plan that includes some of your employees' ideas.

A survey provides employees the opportunity to voice their opinions and strengthens overall engagement and corporate wellness. As employees see their ideas implemented, they feel integral to the team's success. Consider conducting surveys throughout the year on various topics in order to receive constant feedback. It is a win-win: employees are given the opportunity to speak up and management is provided with a stream of fresh suggestions.

This chapter provides guidelines for conducting effective employee engagement surveys.

When to Conduct Surveys

As a management team, if you find yourselves asking, "What is best for the employees?" or "How might this change impact morale?" take the time to conduct a short survey on the topic.

For example, at Actualize, we were experiencing low turnout for social events, so we decided to ask employees their preferences on the where, what, and when of each event. We then listened to the survey responses and chose events based on the majority preference. As a result, we have increased our participation rates to close to full attendance for all events. Our approach is to survey year-round because we are curious about what our team is feeling, thinking, and wanting. We could plan, ponder, and try to assume what will work; however, by asking for input, we foster a sense of community, which in turn enhances feelings of involvement and belonging. Direct feedback from employees is so much better than guessing!

Steps for Effective Surveys

As I mentioned before, an effective survey requires more than just tossing a few questions out to employees. It requires careful planning, execution, and follow-up. We use a five-step survey process at Actualize, discussed in more detail on the following pages:

1. Create
2. Announce
3. Execute
4. Analyze and implement
5. Follow up

1. Create the Survey

A useful survey starts with the right length, right format, and right questions.

Right Length

This is one case where more is not better. Keep surveys short. Our annual employee satisfaction survey at Actualize used to be more than forty questions. That was too many questions for employees to deal with, however, and it was challenging to decipher the results to discover what employees truly desired. In the last two years, we have streamlined this survey down to just six questions. Now employees are more willing to provide answers, which are then much easier to tally and analyze.

Right Format

Surveys are often entirely made up of multiple-choice questions. There is nothing wrong with multiple-choice questions, but if you use them you should make sure to also provide space for commentary. We have found that when we provide space to formulate responses freely, employees reveal many more insights. The most helpful and complete answers open-ended questions.

Right Questions

Take the time to carefully consider the questions you want to ask. What do you really want to find out? And if you find that out, will you be able to act on the information? If not, leave that question out. Include questions that get right to the heart of what you want to know about employee wants, needs, and experiences, and review those questions with several different team members to ensure they're clear. As we discussed before, listening and not making assumptions is a key success factor.

For example, Actualize asks employees the following six questions on our annual survey:

1. What is your favorite thing about working for the firm?

2. What would you like to see the firm accomplish in the upcoming year?

3. What project have you enjoyed working on most while with us, and what were the main factors making it enjoyable?

4. What aspects of your role and activities at our firm motivate you?

5. Are there any aspects of the company that make your life or job more difficult than they need to be? If so, please list them as well as what we could do to remove these obstacles.

6. Any other feedback you would like to share? Any other suggestions?

More recently, we added a brief mid-year survey asking three questions:

1. What are 2–4 suggestions you would like to share to enhance our firm?

2. What inspired or motivated you the most in the first six months?

3. Any other feedback you would like to share? Any other suggestions?

It took us some time and not-great questions to get to this short, useful list of clear questions. For example, our previous employee survey consisted of multiple-choice questions, which were guiding their responses versus letting them freely speak their feelings, and therefore did not provide the robust level of detail we receive in response to the open-ended questions. Give yourself some time to experiment and tweak your questions as needed. If you do not receive meaningful feedback to help you make changes or confirm satisfaction, consider changing what you are asking and how.

2. Announce the Survey

Don't just spring a survey on your employees. Let them know ahead of time that you will be sending out a survey for their feedback. Tell them the date to expect it and how many days they will have to respond, making sure to provide enough time for them to fully complete the survey. Also, tell them why their feedback is important. As we discussed earlier, it is important to start with the why. In Simon Sinek's book *Start with Why: How Great Leaders Inspire Everyone to Take Action*, he explains, "Very few people or companies can clearly articulate WHY they do WHAT they do. By WHY I mean your purpose, cause or belief—WHY does your company exist? WHY do you get out of bed every morning? And WHY should anyone care? People don't buy WHAT you do, they buy WHY you do it."[39]

By providing a heads-up about the survey, you give employees the chance to start thinking about how they feel about their work and the organization. It also shows you treat the survey with respect by giving employees the same considerations as if it were a new project.

Senior leadership also needs to send a clear message of the survey's importance and purpose. Assure the employees that management will carefully read all responses and will report back with findings and implementation plans. Remember to communicate that the survey responses will remain anonymous. These messages from leadership help make employees stakeholders, aiding in higher levels of participation and more candid responses.

3. Execute the Survey

Now that you have the questions ready, what tool should you use to execute the survey? You can hire an outside firm to conduct the survey, or use one of the many online survey tools on the market such as SurveyGizmo, SurveyMonkey, Zoho Survey, or a form in Google Docs. These online tools manage the distribution of questions and collection of responses. As survey answers come in, you can see the data in ready-made reports that are usually available online and in PDF format. Most tools also allow you to customize reports for more detailed analysis, and the data can be exported to other analysis and reporting tools such as spreadsheets.

Surveys don't need to be a big budget item if you take the time up front to explore these different options.

4. Analyze and Implement Suggestions

After you have gathered the data, it's time to analyze it. There are different ways of handling analysis, but the following two tips have consistently been effective for me:

- **Group responses into themes:** As you read all the responses, note what themes emerge. Group data according to those themes so you can more easily understand the data and provide results.

- **Cross-check your analysis:** Have someone who is not close to the data also review and analyze it. If your budget allows, consider using an outside firm for this; otherwise, if Team

A responded to the survey, have someone from Team B analyze the results.

You can then take this data analysis and share the results with employees and other leaders. Don't let this valuable information just stay with management! When you communicate survey results openly and in a timely manner, you build trust and set the tone for employees to provide continued honest feedback and ideas for improvement. No matter what the results are, be honest about them. Don't try to position results to be better or worse than they are; that is of no help to your employees or the organization.

One of the most effective ways to share survey data is through action-planning meetings. In those meetings, give individual employees responsibility for coming up with the best solutions to implement suggested organizational changes, giving them ownership in the process.

Take feedback seriously and implement changes where possible. Rather than trying to improve all dimensions at once, focus on only one or two critical items with each survey cycle (this is another reason to ideally conduct a survey more than once a year). Each manager should facilitate their team's action-planning meeting and ensure action is taken on suggestions (e.g., "Our lowest score was on transparency. Why do you think that is? Who has an idea of what we could do to improve in this area?"). It is also important to be transparent about the changes that are not feasible or practical, and to explain why. If employees know why, they are less likely to be upset about their suggestions not being taken into consideration. This open communication increases engagement by showing employees that management is listening to them.

As Walt Disney believed, "Employees will only complain or make suggestions three times on the average without a response. After that they conclude that if they don't keep quiet they will be thought to be troublemakers or that management doesn't care." Remember the discussion on active listening earlier in the book? Survey responses are absolutely one of the things that leaders must listen *and respond to* in order to keep communication open and effective.

5. Follow Up on Survey

After the action plans are in place, remember to communicate on executed items. Firms often fail to loop employees in when items on the list are complete, so employees will assume that the action items were not done or didn't matter. Letting the team in on the positive progress of the action plans they developed continues to mold a culture of possibility, unity, and open communication. Each individual brings knowledge and value to the table, so notice it, listen to and acknowledge them, and act on their suggestions whenever possible.

> **"In the long history of humankind those who learned to collaborate and improvise most effectively have prevailed."**
>
> **—Charles Darwin**

Conclusion

Employees are the beating heart of an organization, so organizations that want to honor and leverage their employees will take the time to gather employees' opinions and preferences.

Steps for Conducting Effective Surveys

1. Create

2. Announce

3. Execute

4. Analyze and implement

5. Follow up

MIND-EXPANDING EXPERIENCES

Personal

Reflect on the surveys your organization conducts over the course of the year. Make a list of the ones you can remember, then answer the following questions.

1. If you are privy to the data, do you feel like you obtained the information you were requesting?

2. If you only took the surveys, do you feel like the questions allowed you to truly express how you think and feel?

3. Was there follow-up after the surveys?

4. What would you do differently to ensure all voices are heard in employee surveys?

If your organization did not conduct any surveys, what feedback would you provide about the overall situation at the firm to your leadership team? Write a memo and consider submitting your feedback for consideration.

Team

In your immediate team or group and using a survey tool to ensure it is anonymous, ask 3–5 open-ended questions about how your team or group can collaborate more effectively or what they enjoy most about their jobs. Ensure to implement the agreed-upon strategies.

Culture Infusion

Commit to conducting at least 2–4 surveys throughout the year to check in with your employees. As discussed earlier, at Actualize we do a mid-year survey and a short annual survey to gauge overall team satisfaction, and then we sprinkle in surveys throughout the year to ask questions about social and wellness events and other areas where we are questioning which path to take. If I find myself asking, "I wonder what others would like to do?" I will typically send out a quick survey. Our team knows that we take their feedback seriously, so we have a high response rate.

PRINCIPLE 8

Align Goals to Rewarding Performance

Nothing can stop the man with the right mental attitude from achieving his goal; nothing on earth can help the man with the wrong mental attitude.

—Thomas Jefferson

We all have our own stories about successes and failures with the goals we have set over the years. To be honest, the water-cooler talk around goals is usually about how annoying Human Resources is about the process for goals and reviews! How many times have you felt as though your manager was just checking the box to talk to you about your goals and get your review done? In many cases, this is a last-minute dreaded task for all involved, even when goals are tied to raises and bonuses.

Instead of focusing on the negative perceptions of goal setting, this principle will help you take goal setting seriously and with a positive attitude, viewing goals as a way for leadership to cultivate inspiration. The idea is to actually spend time with your team on creating meaningful and achievable goals that are aligned with the areas in which each person excels and is most interested. Then, work with each person to create a plan that will align their personal goals with the firm's goals, while ensuring they are focusing on their areas of expertise and interest.

At Actualize, we start with setting our annual firm-wide goals, which then allows for individual goals to be linked with the firm's goals in order to create a win-win situation: individual goals provide important individual motivation *and* help move the company forward.

For years, we had a goal-setting process for employees that offered little guidance; we would only look at their goals in our biannual review process. Now, our structure encourages our people to use their goals as a working document of their progress throughout the year, similar to a personal status report.

Before, we wondered why employees didn't engage with the process. Then we streamlined the process and structured it around the 3P's we were already using to guide firm-wide performance: our People, Projects, and Profitability. It has been beneficial to have a laser focus for all our firm's initiatives by setting firm-wide goals in each of these areas. For instance, Projects goals are around client growth and providing excellent customer satisfaction. The Profitability goals denote our revenue and utilization. Now, our team members can choose how they can help us achieve our overall goals by choosing their own goals for each of the 3P's. Given that our people are our best asset, we have a subset of the first P called the 3A's, which helps foster inspiration in goal setting:

1. Accountability

2. Acumen

3. Aspiration

Let's explore each of the 3A's.

1. Accountability

We advocate bidirectional accountability, which helps employees know they are part of a team in all decisions and leads to satisfied team members. From the time team members begin employment with Actualize, we discuss how we will support them and take accountability for ensuring their success. However, they also must take accountability for letting us know what they want, what is not working well for them, and what they enjoy most. When management and team members take accountability in their roles at work, we stop blaming the politics, culture, or boss and instead get clear on what we truly want. When leaders have this clarity, we can together formulate goals with our team members to inspire them to do fulfilling work. Accountability goals could include submitting time and expense reports on time, or choosing things that you are personally taking accountability for within the firm. For example, I take accountability for organizing and planning our social and cause- related events.

When the entire firm is aligned on accountability, the focus shifts. For example, maybe you are frustrated with a complicated process and have an idea to streamline it. Instead of complaining to co-workers about how the process is broken, set a goal to develop a proposal noting what is working now and how it can be enhanced.

In Daniel H. Pink's book, *A Whole New Mind*, he suggests asking, "Is there one thing I can do tomorrow in my own domain to make things a little better?"[40] Or maybe you have a difficult relationship with a co-worker; set a goal to find ways to relate positively instead of gossiping.

Accountability also means recognizing when you need to apologize. I frequently use Goulston's "Power Apology" from his book *Just Listen*. It consists of four R's: Remorse, Restitution, Rehabilitation, and Requesting forgiveness.[41] For example, I was working on a data-intensive project and I was impatient and brash with a team member. The next day, I took accountability for losing my patience. I started my apology with Remorse: "I know I was brash yesterday; I was honestly more frustrated with the project than you." Moving to Restitution, "I know I hurt your feelings and I know this project is challenging. I am going to take the lead and personally finish the work." Then to Rehabilitation, "I recognize that I can easily lose patience and I am working on pausing versus reacting in tense situations." Finally, requesting forgiveness, "Are you able to forgive me for upsetting you? I am truly sorry." I also like to add humor and then playfully say as I do with my children when I mess up, "Can we have a do-over?" That typically makes them laugh or smile. In this example, my apology allowed us to move forward versus getting stuck. My team member appreciated the humility in that apology.

We have seen that as our team members take accountability for their own happiness at work, we are more focused on adding value and bringing opportunities to the table to expand our success.

2. Acumen

When setting inspiring goals, "acumen" means working with your team on what they want to learn more about in relation to their area of expertise. Because Actualize is a boutique consulting firm, we coach our team members to make every effort to become the expert to ensure they are adding value and are the go-to person in their specialty. We ask them to determine what they can do to become better known, such as conducting internal training, mentoring others, writing articles, or speaking at conferences. As the saying goes, you learn something new every day, and learning keeps you young. It will also help you be more inspired. Not only should you encourage your employees in their personal and professional development, but you as a manager should be working on your own development.

For years, I was stuck in "doing" mode and not able to see a bigger picture or different ways of running the internal operations at Actualize. I began to feel I was adding no value. Then I decided to go to seminars, learn from new sources, and read books on leadership and human psychology. With each learning opportunity, I would find a nugget to bring back and implement at the firm. This active learning is how I was able to help slowly build a culture our employees want to be a part of.

Acumen also applies to personal interests and goals. If your company has a training allowance, you can encourage employees to spend a portion of the money on something more personal versus only professional development. That will show your commitment to them and the organization's wellness culture.

You might be surprised to hear that employees might need an extra push to use training money for their personal growth. I had an employee that never used her training budget and I realized that she was so focused on the daily routine and work that she was not taking any time for herself outside of work or her duties as a mom. I finally put my foot down and told her that her bonus would be impacted if she did not use her training allowance. That sounds odd, yet I knew it would be good for her. I opened the training idea up to more personal items that were of interest to her, and she was energized by the training she did finally take. It is amazing what you will experience if you get out and try something new or take a class from a new teacher.

Focusing on acumen through continuous learning allows us to see different approaches and viewpoints outside of the day-to-day grind. The supervisors and I work with team members to set goals to develop their skills in an area of expertise, and as a result they find their work more enjoyable and rewarding. We guide them towards becoming indispensable in the workplace.

3. Aspiration

The third step of setting inspirational goals is to encourage all personnel within your organization from top to bottom to discover the aspirations that will light them up by determining their preferences for career and personal life. Many times, I will ask, "What do you aspire to achieve? What do you desire out of your career?" Once they focus on the aspects that excite them professionally and personally, they can then link their goals to areas they most enjoy. It is important to look at your personal life as well to ensure you have an outlet for all the things you gain pleasure from. As Malcolm Forbes said, "I think the foremost quality—

there's no success without it—is really loving what you do. If you love it, you do it well, and there's no success if you don't do well what you're working at."

Steve Jobs frequently would say, "If you are working on something that you really care about, you don't have to be pushed. The vision pulls you." I know "do what you love" sounds cliché, yet if we focus on the areas that bring joy, there's no doubt we will be successful and advance in our work. You probably won't love all aspects of your work, so finding a focus you love can help make other parts of your job more enjoyable.

For example, maybe you love giving back to the community and your firm needs someone to lead the next community service event. Signing up for that role can help balance your work and personal interests. Or you can set a goal to lead more community service events or to plan an event that's different than any your company has done before. Or maybe you prefer working with people on career development, so set a goal to manage more people or develop a leadership program.

Performance Reviews

As I mentioned previously, we streamlined the performance review process at Actualize. Not only did we change the way we set our goals, but we also enhanced the review cycle, and we saved money by eliminating the automated workflow system we had implemented. It was cumbersome and the complicated workflow the system offered was not necessary. Given our firm has less than fifty full-time employees, we were able to instead use our cloud technology to set up a folder structure in which all who need to can readily review the goal files and add performance notes throughout the year. From an administrative perspective, I am able to drop kudos, 360 feedbacks, client satisfaction notes, and so on directly into the file. The goals, performance, and career plan are stored in one document. We formally conduct reviews and pay bonuses every six months.

This process ensures the supervisor, employee, and I are in constant communication and also on the same page, actively engaged in their success and supportive of the individual's personal goals and aspirations. Additionally, as the lead of the goal and performance processes, I make it a point each review cycle to check in with supervisors and any employees who require extra attention. I also speak to each employee during their goal setting at the beginning of each year. These conversations are invaluable for giving appropriate feedback, coaching, and attention at an individual level. I believe taking this time is critical to our positively infused culture. Our people know I genuinely care about their careers and about them personally. Granted, I am afforded this luxury given our size.

Performance reviews should be interactive in order to ensure appropriate feedback is given. We do this at Actualize by including a comments section in which both the subordinate and their supervisor write an overall assessment of the six-month period, including a list of three strengths and three areas of improvement to work on in the next period. This process ensures two-way communication. Below is an example of how one team member successfully utilized my focus on wanting the best for everyone.

**REAL-LIFE EXAMPLE FROM AN
ACTUALIZE SENIOR CONSULTANT**

"Kerry makes it a point to continue learning about employees' career goals, development, and personal interests. She schedules time with me to discuss these items or just catch up as friends. I know I can always go to her if I have an issue or goal or am in need of some advice. She looks out for my long-range growth and satisfaction.

When my manager asked me to work on a project for my former employer, I said I would work with them for a short time to help our company position ourselves well at that client. Kerry recognized that being on that project long-term was not where I ultimately wanted to be. She made sure to acknowledge my willingness to assist with the project but ensured it would remain a short-term assignment.

I truly feel Kerry is focused on developing my career and has my best interests at heart as an employee and as a person."

Rewarding for Performance

Although much of the success in meeting goals is up to each employee, the organization also plays an important role. Managers need to support their employees in setting inspirational goals, and the organization needs to then reward employees for work well done towards those goals. Following are some ways to provide appropriate and effective rewards.

Culture Infusion

- **Tenure awards:** Give employees an award for reaching a designated number of years of service. Examples include monetary awards, gifts, additional vacation time, or other creative rewards. Employees want—and deserve—to be valued for their loyalty to your firm.

- **Recognition program:** Implement a way for peers to recognize each other. For example, a "star player" award allows employees to nominate their peers by providing management with information on why the person should be recognized. The rewards can be monetary or prize based, depending on what works best for your firm. Written kudos are another way everyone in the firm can highlight excellent performance. Empower a culture in which kudos are encouraged via email blast to all employees in the firm or to your immediate team, or if you do a newsletter you can solicit kudos for each edition.

- **Performance bonuses:** Provide monetary rewards based on annual or biannual (or other appropriate frequency) performance reviews.

- **Profit-sharing or stock options:** Give employees monetary payouts based on company profits and/or ownership via stock options. These incentives provide employees extra motivation to support the success of the company both in and beyond their own job role.

- **Sales and referral incentives:** Provide monetary payouts as reward for bringing in new work or referring strong candidates who are then hired by the firm. This helps build a culture of shared growth and connection.

- **Work towards a shared mission:** As we focus on our people and our client service at Actualize, we make that our mission in all our discussions and we celebrate our people and client success. In Daniel H. Pink's book *Drive*, he discusses how a shared mission creates a team bond: "The more that people share a common cause—whether it's creating something insanely great, outperforming an outside competitor, or even changing the world—the more your group will do deeply satisfying and outstanding work."[42]

Conclusion

Many people sigh at the mention of setting goals, but leaders can turn goal setting into a rewarding experience by focusing on personal accountability, acumen, and aspiration aligned with corporate goals. Goals shouldn't be boring requirements to just check off a list; they should be interesting, important to the employee, and even a stretch or an adventure.

In order for goals to be effective, meaningful performance reviews should happen on a regular basis. We encourage our team members to track progress similar to a status report and review accomplishments monthly with their supervisor to enable a smooth review process. That way, when their performance review rolls around, they don't have to worry about remembering all they have accomplished in the review period. And, to bring the

> "It is only in adventure that some people succeed in knowing themselves— in finding themselves."
>
> **—André Gide**

goals full circle, it is important to also set up a generous reward system.

Align goals to rewarding performance by:

- Working with your team on connecting goals to the 3A's: accountability, acumen, and aspiration;

- Streamlining your performance review process to best align with your organization's needs; and

- Rewarding your team members for high performance.

MIND-EXPANDING EXPERIENCES

Personal

Write down your answers to the following questions:

1. What do you like about your goal-setting and performance-review processes?
2. What could be changed?
3. How could the processes be improved to gain more interactive and two-way communication year-round?
4. How could you incorporate more accountability, acumen, and aspiration in your processes?

Team

How do you get your employees started with the creative process of setting inspirational goals? Before employees set their goals for the coming year, have them complete this simple exercise to get clear on what they want to be doing. They can choose which answers they want to share with you.

Ask them to take time to reflect and mindfully complete the following:

1. Make a list of all of your job functions.

2. Highlight the ones that bring you the most joy. Keep this list for reference.

3. Highlight the ones you excel at. Keep this list for reference.

4. Honestly answer the following questions (feel free to use your lists from #2 and #3 above to spark your thinking):

    a. What inspires you?

    b. Who inspires you professionally?

    c. What is your favorite thing about your work?

    d. What excites you personally? At work?

    e. In what ways could the passions you pursue on a personal level benefit your firm?

    f. What do you want to be doing professionally in five years?

    g. What skills do you want to improve?

    h. What type of project do you want to be on next?

    i. What would you like to help with internally?

    j. What would you like to learn more about internally?

  k. What would you like to help your firm accomplish next year?

  l. What would you like your firm to help you accomplish next year?

  m. What is your favorite thing about working at your firm?

  n. What do you do to ensure balance in your life?

  o. Do you give yourself time to do the things you love most?

5. Review your lists and identify themes or recurring answers. Share with your supervisor.

6. Work with your supervisor to create goals that align with your desires.

This exercise will help employees get excited about the next year, balancing the personal and professional as they create a fresh new set of goals that supports their wellness and job advancement.

Modification for Managers and Executives

This same exercise is also helpful for managers and executives. Because their goals are likely more complex and more directly impacted by the firm's goals, you might hire an executive coach to help work through the exercise with the team as a whole or with each person individually. It is challenging to truly see ourselves without enlisting a third party. Executive coaches help bring clarity by asking even more questions, offering challenges, and generally pushing towards high achievement in a way that works for that specific leader. Some executive coaches are paid specifically to challenge and disagree with their client in order to ensure the client is taking time to formulate decisions versus being reactionary. Abraham Lincoln was one of the rare presidents with a cabinet of political opponents willing to disagree with him. Sporting teams focus on finding superior coaches who push them in order to win. Similarly, organizations are using coaches to guide their leaders towards success. Another alternative is to enlist an internal member from your organization to assist with this process if they have natural leadership and coaching acumen.

Culture Infusion

Align your goal-setting and performance-review processes and streamline them so your team is not dreading the process. Determine ways you can take a similar approach to Actualize's with the 3P's (People, Projects, and Profitability) and the 3A's (Accountability, Acumen, and Aspiration). Ponder what best represents your overall mission and vision.

PRINCIPLE 9

Encourage Team Connection

Whatever affects one directly, affects all indirectly.

—Martin Luther King Jr.

Getting together as a firm helps to reduce stress and build closer relationships, which in turn promotes better teamwork and greater work satisfaction. Plus, the activities can be fun and meaningful! These events are also a great way for leadership to show their support for a culture that prioritizes well-being.

At Actualize, we also encourage employees to participate in activities that support social causes. We believe in sharing our success by giving back in ways that are truly helpful to our local community, and our employees value and look forward to those experiences. We have found that even a small company can have a huge impact when leadership truly cares about making a positive difference.

In this chapter, I share with you some tips for successful employee activities—including cause-related ones—and examples of activities that you might want to try with your own organization.

Employee Social Activities

In keeping with our belief in the importance of fun in our personal and work lives and our goal to encourage team connection, Actualize offers several team social activities outside of the work environment each year. We make sure to involve employees in selecting activities so we can get creative ideas and also do things that our team members actually want to do.

Tips for Successful Employee Social Activities

With a little extra thought and intention, you can help make employee social activities something that the whole firm looks forward to. Use the following tips to guide your planning:

1. **Confirm leadership support:** Remember that these employee social activities are an important part of your company culture. Offer these activities as a perk, a token of your appreciation, and a sign that you care about your employees' well-being and enjoyment.

2. **Survey employees:** Make sure to determine what your employees like to do and allow them to choose. Request their suggestions, then offer those as the options on a survey you send out to them. Ask employees to choose their top two preferences. Select the most popular activity.

3. **Send thank you notes:** Have management write and send a "thank you for attending" note to all employees that also

includes a request for suggestions for the next employee social activity.

4. **Share the fun:** Take pictures/videos and share on social media to celebrate your employees and to inspire other companies. Compile into a video to use as a marketing tool for new recruits. We have a video of our annual retreat on our corporate website and regularly receive positive feedback about it from recruits.

Examples of Employee Social Activities

There are many options for different types of events you might try. Following are a few ideas to get you started:

- **Book club:** This is a great way to read business, leadership, and personal interest books and discuss as a group. At Actualize, we ask everyone to suggest ideas for books, then as a group decide on the next book. We encourage people to attend our meetings even if they have not read the book.

- **House party:** This is perfect if someone from the management team is willing to volunteer their house. Having a low-key party at someone's house allows for a relaxed time and much more socialization. You can have the party catered, hire a band, play games, or have other activities like a cooking contest (and give prizes!).

- **Sporting events:** Choose a sport that the majority of your employees enjoy and attend a sporting event together.

- **Team building:** Hire an outside firm to come in and host a team-building event. Or play a sport together (such as bowling, pool, or laser tag), take a cooking or painting class, or hire an improv company for interactive activities.

- **Company retreat:** Hold an off-site weekend, including some planned activities. Consider a wellness event, a yoga and/or relaxation class, and other activities that provide laughter and connection.

- **Field trips by bus:** Go on a field trip together. Depending upon preferences, consider a wine tour, a scavenger hunt, sightseeing in a local city, or an outing to a nearby theater (shows, comedy club, etc.). Traveling by bus gives employees a chance to enjoy the trip together without needing to plan their own transportation.

- **Contests:** Organize online contests around the football season or March Madness for basketball. As mentioned previously, have Lunch and Play sessions with simple game tournaments and use company swag as prizes. Contests encourage friendly competition that helps folks get to know each other better. It brings out friendly banter and really helps everyone open up.

For additional ideas, ask your employees to get creative (you can even provide a prize for a team that comes up with an idea that gets the most votes) or hire an outside firm to plan.

As discussed in Principle 2: Prioritize Personal Wellness, play is important both personally and professionally. When we allow ourselves time to play, we expand our minds to see a new perspective. For example, while hosting twenty-two people for Thanksgiving, I felt zero hosting stress. Why? I was playing, singing, and dancing with my guests. Typically, I would have been worried, stressed, and agitated that the house was getting dirty; instead, I was having so much fun that all that fell to the wayside.

In his book *Essentialism*, Greg McKeown dedicates an entire chapter to the value of play. He includes this great quote from Edward M. Hallowell (from his book *Shine: Using Brain Science to Get the Best From Your People*):

> Play stimulates the parts of the brain involved in both careful, logical reasoning and carefree, unbound exploration. [For example,] Columbus was out at play when it dawned on him that the world was round. Newton was at play in his mind when he saw the apple tree and suddenly conceived the force of gravity. Watson and Crick were playing with possible shapes of the DNA molecule when they stumbled upon the double helix. Shakespeare played with iambic pentameter his whole life. Mozart barely lived a waking moment when he was not at play. Einstein's thought experiments are brilliant examples of the mind invited to play.[43]

Make sure to keep play in mind as you plan employee social events—it will benefit your people and the company as a whole!

Cause-Related Employee Activities

When we give back, we share a deeper sense of connection. That is why we also encourage cause-related employee activities—those that enhance corporate social responsibility (CSR). CSR originally came about as a way to counteract damage that large corporations did to the environment and the communities around them. People assumed that companies that actually made a profit would in some way be harmful, so the companies needed a way to balance out that image. Over time, however, companies began changing their business models to be socially responsible from the inside out—so CSR is now more about adding good to the world than compensating for something bad they have done.

At Actualize, CSR plays a critical role in our business strategy. Remember our tagline, "Our expertise and commitment driving your success"? Our core purpose is to deliver results for our clients, which includes helping the communities our clients are part of.

Before you jump into organizing a company donation to a charity or leading a community benefit event, take the time to get clear on *why* your company is doing this. As you can imagine, some companies just do something positive for the community because it makes them look good. Make sure your organization is actually interested in helping, or those actions won't feel good to the recipients or your employees.

A corporate culture that prioritizes wellness and employee happiness will likely be willing to extend that focus to the greater community. As Daniel Goleman said in his books *Focus* and *Emotional Intelligence*, "One aspect of wisdom is having a very wide horizon which doesn't center on ourselves,"[44] or even on our group or organization. He notes that giving back without needing anything in return is a true sign of wisdom, no matter whether the form of giving back is creative, social, personal, or financial.

Check in with leadership to make sure they are on board and willing to use company resources (money, time, energy) for CSR or cause-related activities.

TIPS for Successful Cause-Related Activities

Once you have confirmed leadership support, you can follow these steps to set your CSR in motion:

1. **Align activities with employee and corporate goals:** As I mentioned in the previous chapter, it's important that your people align their goals with their personal and professional aspirations, and with corporate goals. The same goes for CSR activities. For example, if your team is working on healthy eating, consider providing healthy lunches to a local shelter.

2. **Survey employees:** Give your people information on several different CSR options that clearly show how they can make a positive difference. Ask your team members to choose their favorite option or to provide other suggestions. Make sure to provide individual- and team-level opportunities. This allows you to listen to what employees actually want to do, so they will be more engaged and authentic in helping their community. Do your best to give your people time and resources to carry out their first or second choice.

3. **Take action:** Plan and carry out the activities, either as individuals or teams based on the activity. Make sure leadership sends the message that this time away from the office is fully supported and the activity is valued by the company.

4. **Report:** Plan a brown-bag lunch or other meeting for employees to come together to share about their CSR activities. Ask them to describe:

a. What activity they did

b. How it felt to them

c. What responses they got

d. Whether they feel it should stay on the corporate list of CSR options

    Follow this sharing with a brief discussion of additional options for future CSR activities.

5. **Share on social media:** Show your team in action, giving back. Encourage your team members to also take pictures of their CSR activities and share on social media. This sharing could spark some great ideas for other companies to also get involved in community support.

Examples of Cause-Related Employee Activities

There are many opportunities to help out others while also providing your employees with a meaningful experience. At Actualize, we encourage employees to work together as teams to create and take part in CSR activities and events. This extra teamwork is a great experience for the employees and benefits the company as well, giving teams practice in working together effectively—all for a good cause. Definitely a win-win situation! Some options for cause-related activities follow.

Charity Events

Participate as a firm in charity events throughout the year. You can make it competitive by forming small groups who each choose their own charity, then have a competition to see who can raise the most money and provide the best support to their organization of choice. This allows you to focus on more than one charity at a time and acts as a team-building exercise. Another option is to choose one local charity to support year-round and encourage your employees to help at various volunteer activities throughout the year. If your firm is larger, consider storing all the charity options in an online portal so individual teams can select which charity/team-building opportunity they want to select.

Community Support

Actualize goes the extra mile to give a little something back to the community we live in. For example:

- Providing shoes to a local business that supports the homeless in getting jobs
- Providing lunches to a local shelter
- Supporting a backpack drive for underprivileged school children
- Contributing to holiday food and gift drives
- Supporting a coat drive
- Conducting mock interviews for a homeless shelter facilitating re-entry into the workforce

One of our team members said, "I always feel as though I am getting more out of this type of event than I am giving."

Get Creative

Challenge yourself and your employees to come up with unique ways to give back. For example:

- One of my own passions is to support children's well-being, and when I had the idea to create an activity book to give to children battling cancer, Actualize provided funding. Not only did that project give me a creative boost that I was able to bring to my corporate work, but it also has impacted many children (and adults!) across the country.

- Actualize put together a wellness event for underprivileged school children. We did this as a team and had a blast joining together in a team wellness competition at the event.

- We held a "giving back to ourselves and others" theme one month. I sent daily emails to employees with quotes, cartoons, suggestions, and perks to remind employees to give to themselves as well as others. For example, company swag for employees to give clients as a thank you, a coat drive in which anyone who donated a gently used coat would be entered in a drawing for self-care prizes, reminders to play, and sharing of gratitude.

- To ensure a variety of opportunities to help with giving back while having quality time with our team, I schedule play dates in smaller groups. We have fun together whether we're preparing lunches for the homeless, sharing together in a meal, or participating in a movement session such as yoga.

Conclusion

The people of your company are its greatest asset, and setting up fun and meaningful employee events is a great way to say thank you. These events also help reduce employee stress, and they enhance relationships as employees get to know each other better outside the office.

When your people take part in activities for a social cause, they get to know their co-workers and hone their teamwork skills while giving back to their communities and other organizations that have a positive impact on our world. At the same time, your company's overall culture is enhanced, especially when these activities are also aligned to individual, team, and corporate goals.

No matter the activity, make sure to let your team members help choose the activities, and provide clear support from leadership so they see by example that your organization values connection, play, and reward as well as work.

Tips for Successful Employee Social Activities

1. Confirm leadership support

2. Survey employees

3. Send thank you notes

4. Share the fun

Tips for Successful Cause-Related Employee Activities

1. Align activities with employee and corporate goals

2. Survey employees

3. Take action

4. Report

5. Share on social media

MIND-EXPANDING EXPERIENCES

Personal

Write down your answers to the following questions:

1. When was the last time you participated in an act of giving back, whether planned via your company or at a personal level?

2. How did the event make you feel?

3. Did you feel a sense of connection? If so, how?

4. If you had unlimited time and funds, what would you do to give back?

5. How can you accomplish those goals with the resources you currently have?

Team

Meet with your immediate team and devise a plan to carry out a small act of kindness or giving back. Take plenty of pictures, then report back to your peers and challenge other teams to do the same. Sharing and caring together will bring your team closer to each other.

Culture Infusion

Using your answers to the questions in the Personal section above, how can you enhance your organization's existing social and CSR activities to provide more connection among your team members and your community?

CONCLUSION

Paying It Forward

As we come to the end of this book, I want to bring the ideas here full circle and ask that we apply the relevant principles to our interactions with all those in our lives—co-workers, family, children, significant others, friends, and strangers. I strive to be the same in all areas of my life. I understand work is work and personal is personal, yet I also see how challenging it is to stay balanced if there is no crossover between work and personal. Principle 1 encourages us to provide intentional leadership and lead by example. We can start today, right now, by modeling the behavior that will create and maintain a thriving culture as well as shift personal relationships. For example:

- Listen to understand
- See the positive side
- Have empathy and compassion for others
- Create balance
- Prioritize personal wellness

- Move in some fashion, whether play, walking, yoga, or games with my kids

- Give back

Life ebbs and flows, and through that contrast we gain gratitude for the positive aspects of our life. During the compilation of this book, my childhood best friend passed away suddenly. As I described at the beginning of the book, the near death of a close friend helped set my transition in motion, but this time it was for real and it hit me hard. For the first time, I allowed sadness and tears to flow naturally while practicing the principles I speak of. I was able to allow myself to feel the death of my friend however I was feeling it, and was then able to rebound in a healthy way. I miss her every day and take time to live life even more fully with this reminder that each day is a new day, a new adventure. Going back to the Helen Keller quote I mentioned earlier in the book, "Life is either a daring adventure or nothing at all."

MIND-EXPANDING EXPERIENCES

Personal

Write down a list of ways you can pay forward what you have learned in this book. For the next week, do at least one thing each day to pay forward your learning.

Team/Culture Infusion

How will you take the Culture Infusion principles and incorporate them daily for your personal well-being and to create a thriving organizational culture? Take time to identify one way you will incorporate each principle.

- Principle 1. Provide intentional leadership
- Principle 2: Prioritize personal wellness
- Principle 3: Insist on a healthy work/life balance
- Principle 4: Practice effective communication
- Principle 5: Handle conflict directly, openly, and immediately
- Principle 6: Focus on your people
- Principle 7: Regularly conduct employee surveys
- Principle 8: Align goals to rewarding performance
- Principle 9: Encourage team connection

GRATITUDE

I express my gratitude to the following people. To each of you who have touched my life, I believe I learn from each of you and all experiences. Thank you from the center of my heart. To those who are just meeting me, I welcome getting to know you and working with you in the near future.

Audrey and Blaine Elam, my kids and wisest teachers. Your bright and joyous spirits inspire me to always be my best self for our highest good and for all those around us.

My dad, Al Wekelo, for being a sounding board for creating and sharing all my work. For the back-cover picture and coining the term "Mind-Expanding Experiences"—that label brought clarity on deep levels.

My mom, Sandra Stowers, for teaching me about hard work and showing me how to be a woman in business. You allowed me years of working in our family's business in which I learned how to fairly and successfully lead the operations and people at Actualize.

Culture Infusion

My brother, Chad Wekelo, for believing in and trusting my vision for our culture at Actualize. You are a role model for striving for perfection. I have been honored to support you and am grateful now to share our cultural success with others.

Bo Elam, my kids' dad and my life partner, for a life of flow and ease that has allowed me space to create. You are the one we call on to make all be magically okay in our world.

My great-grandparents, Cecil and Pauline, and my grandparents, Bill, Gloria, Ray, and Marge, for instilling the foundation that family comes first. I also learned the value of education, working hard, and always taking time for *play*.

Denise and Theresa, my internal team at Actualize since 2006, for your dedication and commitment. There is nothing we cannot accomplish as a team because we act like a family.

Joe Burnham, for your unconditional love and support.

My friends with whom I share spiritual and soul-level connections, your loving kindness and acceptance has encouraged me to be my authentic self.

The Actualize team, past and present, for acting as a playground to explore the principles in *Culture Infusion*. Without each of you, this book would not be possible.

Matt Seu, our other partner at Actualize, for your forever support.

John Harvey, my long-term mentor, for seeing my gifts before I saw them and gracefully guiding me on my way. Thank you for supporting me at Actualize and our other family business, and through the writing of all my books.

My teachers Rolf Gates and Sonia Choquette, for paving the way and giving me the tools to serve others to their highest good.

My editors—Starla King, Heidi King, and Amy Scott—for each of your talents in bringing this book to its best state for our readers.

RESOURCES

Books

Reading can bring you insights in your personal life and professional life. Those listed here are books that I continue to go back to for reference and quotes in my daily life. There are many leadership books on the market; the books below are more about the attitude you are bringing to work.

The Arbinger Institute. *Leadership and Self-Deception: Getting Out of the Box.* San Francisco: Berrett-Koehler, 2000.

Carnegie, Dale. *How to Win Friends and Influence People.* New York: Simon & Schuster, 1981.

Choquette, Sonia. *Your 3 Best Super Powers: Meditation, Imagination & Intuition.* New York: Hay House, 2016.

Covey, Stephen R. *The 7 Habits of Highly Effective People.* New York: Simon & Schuster, 1989.

Cramer, Kathryn D. *Lead Positive: What Highly Effective Leaders See, Say, and Do.* San Francisco: Jossey-Bass & Pfeiffer Imprints, Wiley, 2014.

Frankl, Viktor. *Man's Search for Meaning.* Boston: Beacon Press, 1992.

Gates, Rolf, and Katrina Kenison. *Meditations from the Mat: Daily Reflections on the Path of Yoga.* New York: Anchor Books, 2002.

Gibran, Kahlil. *The Prophet.* New York: Knopf, 1952.

Gladwell, Malcolm. *Blink: The Power of Thinking Without Thinking.* New York: Little, Brown and Co., 2005.

Godin, Seth. *Linchpin: Are You Indispensable?* New York: Portfolio, 2010.

Goleman, Daniel. *Emotional Intelligence: Why It Can Matter More Than IQ.* New York: Bantam Books, 1995.

Goulston, Mark. *Just Listen.* New York: American Management Association, 2010.

Hallowell, Edward M. *Shine: Using Brain Science to Get the Best from Your People.* Boston: Harvard Business Review Press, 2011.

Huffington, Arianna. *Thrive: The Third Metric to Redefining Success and Creating a Life of Well-Being, Wisdom, and Wonder.* New York: Harmony Books, 2014.

Loehr, Jim, and Tony Schwartz. *The Power of Full Engagement: Managing Energy, Not Time, Is the Key to High Performance and Personal Renewal.* New York: Free Press, 2003.

Manning, Harley, and Kerry Bodine. *Outside In: The Power of Putting Customers at the Center of Your Business.* Boston: Houghton Mifflin Harcourt, 2012.

Marquardt, Michael. *Leading with Questions: How Leaders Find the Right Solutions by Knowing What to Ask.* San Francisco: Jossey-Bass, 2005.

McKeown, Greg. *Essentialism: The Disciplined Pursuit of Less.* New York: Crown Business, 2014.

Pink, Daniel H. *A Whole New Mind: Why Right-Brainers Will Rule the Future.* New York: Riverhead Books, 2006.

Rock, David. *Your Brain at Work: Strategies for Overcoming Distraction, Regaining Focus, and Working Smarter All Day Long.* New York: Harper Business, 2009.

Ruiz, don Miguel. *The Four Agreements: A Practical Guide to Personal Freedom.* San Rafael, CA: Amber-Allen Publishers, 1997.

Sinek, Simon. *Start with Why: How Great Leaders Inspire Everyone to Take Action.* New York: Portfolio, 2009.

Tan, Chade-Meng. *Joy on Demand: The Art of Discovering the Happiness Within.* New York: HarperOne, 2016.

———. *Search Inside Yourself: The Unexpected Path to Achieving Happiness (and World Peace).* New York: HarperOne, 2012.

Tavris, Carol, and Elliot Aronson. *Mistakes Were Made (But Not by Me): Why We Justify Foolish Beliefs, Bad Decisions, and Hurtful Acts.* Orlando: Harcourt, 2007.

Thich Nhat Hanh. *The Art of Communicating*. New York: HarperOne, 2013.

Waitley, Denis. *The Psychology of Winning*. Chicago: Nightingale-Conant Corp., 1987.

Zukav, Gary. *The Seat of the Soul*. New York: Simon & Schuster, 1990.

Online Content

Bloom, Nicholas, James Liang, John Roberts, and Zhichun Jenny Ying. "Does Working from Home Work? Evidence from a Chinese Experiment." *The Quarterly Journal of Economics* (2015): 165–218. doi:10.1093/qje/qjuo32.

Brown, Stuart. "Play Is More Than Just Fun." Filmed May 2008. TED video, 26:42. Posted 2008. https://www.ted.com/talks/stuart_brown_says_play_is_more_than_fun_it_s_vital?language=en.

The Center for Generational Kinetics. "Generational Breakdown: Info about All of the Generations." Accessed November 1, 2016. http://genhq.com/faq-info-about-generations/.

Gorman, James. "Scientists Hint at Why Laughter Feels So Good." *The New York Times*, September 13, 2011, http://www.nytimes.com/2011/09/14/science/14laughter.html?_r=0.

Harvard Medical School. "Relaxation Techniques: Breath Control Helps Quell Errant Stress Response." Harvard

Health Publications. Last modified March 18, 2016. http://www.health.harvard.edu/mind-and-mood/relaxation-techniques-breath-control-helps-quell-errant-stress-response.

Heathers, James. "Introduction to Vagal Tone." Accessed December 1, 2016. http://joyondemand.com/r/vagal_tone.

The Institute of HeartMath. "The Intelligent Heart." Last modified December 24, 2012. http://www.social-consciousness.com/2012/12/science-of-heart-institute-of-heartmath.html.

The National Institute for Play. "The Science: Overview." Accessed November 1, 2016. http://www.nifplay.org/science/overview/.

The Northwestern MutualVoice Team. "Are Leaders Born or Made?" *Forbes*, March 23, 2015, http://www.forbes.com/sites/northwesternmutual/2015/03/23/are-leaders-born-or-made/#3a331bda7ddf.

Sinek, Simon. "How to Get People to Follow You." Interview by Tom Bilyeu. *Inside Quest* podcast, September 7, 2016. Excerpt "On Millennials in the Workplace." Accessed January 3, 2017. https://www.youtube.com/watch?v=hER0Qp6QJNU&sns=em.

Ecosystem Services Team. "Health and Wellness Benefits of Spending Time in Nature." U.S. Department of Agriculture; Forest Service; and Pacific Northwest Research Station. Accessed November 1, 2016. http://

www.fs.fed.us/pnw/about/programs/gsv/pdfs/health_
and_wellness.pdf.

Other Resources by Kerry Alison Wekelo

To work directly with Kerry and her team, visit www.
actualizeconsulting.com, where you will find expansion on the
Mind-Expanding Experiences and can invite us to come in and
work with your organization. Additionally, Kerry is available for
executive-level coaching.

Zendoway Squeezable Cubes are available at https://
www.amazon.com/Zendoway-ZC4pk-Squeezable-Cubes/dp/
B01ICBFMR4 or directly from Kerry's website: http://www.
zendoway.com/cubes.html.

Audio Relaxations and Guided at Your Desk Movements can
be found at http://www.zendoway.com/relaxation-videos.html.

Kerry is also the author of the following books, all available on
Amazon and www.zendoway.com:

- *Audrey's Journey* Series
- *Loving Kindness*
- *Round and Round Yoga*
- *Blaine's Playful Namaste*
- *If It Does Not Grow, Say No: Eatable Activities for Kids*
- *Let's Do Yoga: Coloring and Activity Book*
- *Pile of Smile Activity Book*
- *Wonders of Your Mind Activity Book for Kids*

ENDNOTES

1. Kahlil Gibran, *The Prophet* (New York: Knopf, 1952).

2. Helen Keller, *The Story of My Life* (1903; repr., New York: Dover, 1996).

3. Andy Crouch, *Culture Making: Recovering Our Creative Calling* (Downers Grove, IL: InterVarsity Press, 2013).

4. The Northwestern MutualVoice Team, "Are Leaders Born or Made?" *Forbes*, March 23, 2015, http://www.forbes.com/sites/northwesternmutual/2015/03/23/are-leaders-born-or-made/#3a331bda7ddf.

5. Carol Tavris and Elliot Aronson, *Mistakes Were Made (But Not by Me): Why We Justify Foolish Beliefs, Bad Decisions, and Hurtful Acts* (Orlando: Harcourt, 2007).

6. Gary Zukav, *The Seat of the Soul* (New York: Simon & Schuster, 1990).

7. Sonia Choquette, *Your 3 Best Super Powers: Meditation, Imagination & Intuition* (New York: Hay House, 2016).

8. HeartMath Institute, "The Heart-Brain Connection," accessed July 1, 2017, https://www.heartmath.org/programs/emwave-self-regulation-technology-theoretical-basis/.

9. Sonia Choquette, *Your 3 Best Super Powers: Meditation, Imagination & Intuition* (New York: Hay House, 2016).

10. Malcolm Gladwell, *Blink: The Power of Thinking Without Thinking* (New York: Little, Brown and Co., 2005).

11. The Center for Generational Kinetics, "Generational Breakdown: Info about All of the Generations," accessed November 1, 2016, http://genhq.com/faq-info-about-generations/.

12. Simon Sinek, "How to Get People to Follow You," interview by Tom Bilyeu, *Inside Quest* podcast, September 7, 2016; excerpt, "On Millennials in the Workplace," accessed January 3, 2017, https://www.youtube.com/watch?v=hER0Qp6QJNU&sns=em.

13. Eleanor Roosevelt, *You Learn by Living* (1960; repr., New York: Harper, 2016).

14. Chade-Meng Tan, *Joy on Demand: The Art of Discovering the Happiness Within* (New York: HarperOne, 2016).

15. The Institute of HeartMath, "The Intelligent Heart," last modified December 24, 2012, http://www.social-consciousness.com/2012/12/science-of-heart-institute-of-heartmath.html.

16. Jim Loehr and Tony Schwartz, *The Power of Full Engagement: Managing Energy, Not Time, Is the Key to High*

Performance and Personal Renewal (New York: Free Press, 2003).

17. David Rock, *Your Brain at Work: Strategies for Overcoming Distraction, Regaining Focus, and Working Smarter All Day Long* (New York: Harper Business, 2009).

18. Herbert Benson with Miriam Z. Klipper, *The Relaxation Response* (New York: William Morrow and Company, 1975).

19. Harvard Medical School, "Relaxation Techniques: Breath Control Helps Quell Errant Stress Response," last modified March 18, 2016, http://www.health.harvard.edu/mind-and-mood/relaxation-techniques-breath-control-helps-quell-errant-stress-response.

20. Rolf Gates and Katrina Kenison, *Meditations from the Mat: Daily Reflections on the Path of Yoga* (New York: Anchor Books, 2002).

21. Stuart Brown, "Play Is More Than Just Fun," filmed May 2008, TED video, 26:42, posted 2008, https://www.ted.com/talks/stuart_brown_says_play_is_more_than_fun_it_s_vital?language=en.

22. The National Institute for Play, "The Science: Overview," accessed November 1, 2016, http://www.nifplay.org/science/overview/.

23. Daniel H. Pink, *A Whole New Mind: Why Right-Brainers Will Rule the Future* (New York: Riverhead Books, 2006).

24. Henry David Thoreau, *Walking* (1851; repr., Value Classic Reprints, 2016).

25. Ecosystem Services Team, "Health and Wellness Benefits of Spending Time in Nature," accessed November 1, 2016, http://www.fs.fed.us/pnw/about/programs/gsv/pdfs/health_and_wellness.pdf.

26. Greg McKeown, *Essentialism: The Disciplined Pursuit of Less* (New York: Crown Business, 2014).

27. don Miguel Ruiz, *The Four Agreements: A Practical Guide to Personal Freedom* (San Rafael, CA: Amber-Allen Publishers, 1997).

28. Ibid.

29. Mark Goulston, *Just Listen* (New York: American Management Association, 2010).

30. Genetic Science Learning Center, "How Cells Communicate During Fight or Flight," accessed July 1, 2017, http://learn.genetics.utah.edu/content/cells/fight_flight/.

31. Henry David Thoreau, *The Journal, 1837–1861* (New York: NYRB Classics, 2011).

32. Derek Sivers, *Anything You Want: 40 Lessons for a New Kind of Entrepreneur* (New York: Portfolio, 2015).

33. Jim Collins, *Good to Great: Why Some Companies Make the Leap and Others Don't* (New York: HarperBusiness, 2001).

34. James Gorman, "Scientists Hint at Why Laughter Feels So Good," *The New York Times*, September 13, 2011, http://www.nytimes.com/2011/09/14/science/14laughter.html?_r=0.

35. Dale Carnegie, *How to Win Friends and Influence People* (New York: Simon & Schuster, 1981).

36. Charles Schwab, *Charles Schwab's New Guide to Financial Independence*, rev. ed. (New York: Crown, 2007).

37. Kathryn D. Cramer, *Lead Positive: What Highly Effective Leaders See, Say, and Do* (San Francisco: Jossey-Bass & Pfeiffer Imprints, Wiley, 2014).

38. Ibid.

39. Simon Sinek, *Start with Why: How Great Leaders Inspire Everyone to Take Action* (New York: Portfolio, 2009).

40. Daniel H. Pink, *A Whole New Mind: Why Right-Brainers Will Rule the Future* (New York: Riverhead Books, 2006).

41. Mark Goulston, *Just Listen* (New York: American Management Association, 2010).

42. Daniel H. Pink, *Drive: The Surprising Truth about What Motivates Us* (New York: Riverhead Books, 2009).

43. Greg McKeown, *Essentialism: The Disciplined Pursuit of Less* (New York: Crown Business, 2014).

44. Daniel Goleman, *Emotional Intelligence: Why It Can Matter More Than IQ* (New York: Bantam Books, 1995); Daniel Goleman, *Focus: The Hidden Driver of Excellence* (New York: HarperCollins, 2013).

CPSIA information can be obtained
at www.ICGtesting.com
Printed in the USA
FFOW03n2243081017
40843FF